ETHIOPIA

A Tourist Paradise

Mohamed Amin • Duncan Willetts

D0191545

**Produced by Camerapix for the
ETHIOPIAN TOURISM COMMISSION**

First published 1996
by Ethiopian Tourism Commission,
P.O. Box 2185,
Addis Ababa, Ethiopia

© Camerapix 1996

This book was designed and produced
for the Ethiopian Tourism Commission by
Camerapix Publishers International,
P.O. Box 45048,
Nairobi, Kenya

ISBN 1 874041 34 2

Edited and designed by Barbara Lawrence Balletto

Colour Separations by Universal Graphics, Singapore.

Printed in Singapore by Tienwah Press.

Half-title: Young and old alike take part with relish in Ethiopia's colourful
Timkat, *or Epiphany, ceremonies. Title page: Eerie yet serene, the craggy peaks*
of the Simien Mountains have attracted and fascinated visitors for centuries.
Contents page: A chain of beautiful lakes in Ethiopia's portion of the Great Rift
Valley add to the splendour of the country.

Contents

Introduction 9

'The New Flower' 12

An Ancient Land 20

The Blue Nile 52

Mountain Majesties 64

Down the Rift Valley 88

Ethiopia in Brief 118

Previous pages: Ancient rock-hewn church at Seqoha in Tigray region.

Below, clockwise from top left: Priest at Debra Damo; Harari matriarch with traditional hairstyle; woman of the mountainous Bale region; young boy from the Omo River valley.

Introduction

Ethiopia is truly a land of contrasts and extremes; a land of remote and wild places. Some of the highest and most stunning places on the African continent are found here, such as the ruggedly-carved steeples and spires of the Simien Mountains, one of UNESCO's World Heritage Sites — and some of the lowest, such as the hot but fascinating Danakil Depression, with its sulphur fumaroles and lunar-like landscape.

One of the most striking geographical features of the country, the Great Rift Valley, is home to a chain of beautiful lakes, around which many of Ethiopia's national parks are centred. The widely varying habitats, which include mountains, lakes, deserts, savannahs, and everything in between, host an astonishing array of wildlife and bird life, many of which are endemic; unique to Ethiopia.

Religion in this fascinating country is unique as well. Many visitors know Ethiopia for its splendid rock-hewn churches and colourful ceremonies, symbolic of the Ethiopian Orthodox Church. Perhaps best known are Lalibela's amazing assemblage of rock churches — often referred to as the 'Eighth Wonder of the World' — but equally wondrous are those carved into cliffside crevices in the mountains of the Tigray region; often reached only by the most determined and devout. Islam, too, has strong and centuries-old roots in the country. Although the religion is particularly epitomized in the romantic walled city of Harar, the elegant minarets of mosques can be seen throughout most of the countryside.

But it is Ethiopia's people who join with the spectacular scenery, abundant fauna and fascinating religions to truly round out the character of this ancient land. Many of the country's large variety of ethnic groups have their own customs, crafts, homes, and unique languages. There are an astonishing eighty-three languages, with 200 dialects: just one more amazing feature of amazing Ethiopia.

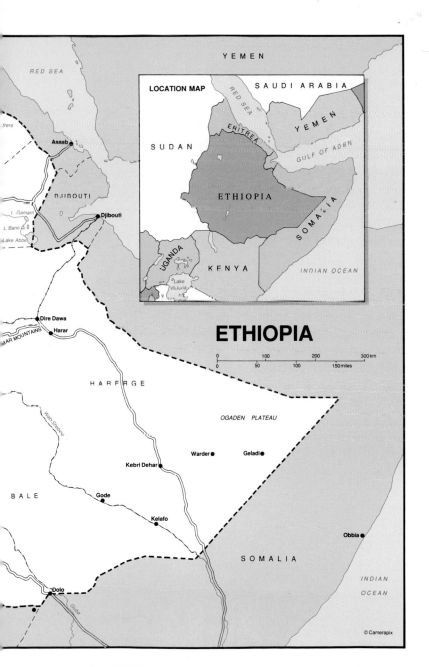

RED SEA

YEMEN

LOCATION MAP

SAUDI ARABIA

RED SEA

ERITREA

YEMEN

SUDAN

GULF OF ADEN

ETHIOPIA

SOMALIA

UGANDA

KENYA

INDIAN OCEAN

Lake Vl.lu.ria

Assab

DJIBOUTI

I. Gamarri

L. Bario

Lake Abbe

Djibouti

Dire Dawa

Harar

MAR MOUNTAINS

ETHIOPIA

0   100   200   300 km
0   50   100   150 miles

HARERGE

OGADEN   PLATEAU

Wabi Shebele

Warder

Geladi

Kebri Dehar

BALE

Gode

Kelafo

Obbia

Dolo

Gibe

SOMALIA

INDIAN OCEAN

© Camerapix

'The New Flower'

Wide tree-lined streets, fine architecture, glorious weather, and the incongruity of donkey trains trolling along the boulevards make Addis Ababa, the Ethiopian capital, a delightful place to explore. It is a city of surprises characterized by remarkable diversity and contrasts.

Addis Ababa's cosy espresso bars and patisseries are reminiscent of Rome and the Mediterranean, and its bustling outdoor markets are colourful reminders of more traditional ways of life. The people, the bursts of music from cafés or shops, the pungent aromas of spicy cooking, of coffee and frankincense, form a unique Ethiopian pastiche.

Dominated by the 3,000-metre (9,840-foot) high Entoto mountains immediately to the north, Ethiopia's largest city has grown at an astonishing speed since it was founded just over a century ago. Covering 250 square kilometres (97 square miles), the city rambles pleasantly across many wooded hillsides and gullies cut through with fast-flowing streams. Despite its proximity to the Equator, its lofty altitude — the third-highest capital in the world — means that it enjoys a mild, Afro-alpine climate.

Addis Ababa was in effect 'founded' in 1886, when Emperor Menelik II's consort, Queen Taytu, asked her husband for a piece of land on which to build a house at the foothills of the Entoto mountains, where Menelik had his camp. The fertile area was the site of hot springs, to which the queen and many of the courtiers spent much of their time travelling. Menelik agreed.

In the same year Queen Taytu gave the settlement its name: Addis Ababa, literally meaning 'New Flower' in Amharic. For several years Menelik and his courtiers divided their time between

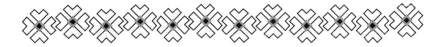

Entoto and the new settlement, but by around 1891 Addis Ababa had definitely become the more important of the two, emerging as the unquestioned capital of the realm.

From its inception Addis Ababa was clustered around two main centres: the palace to the east and the market, with Saint George's Church, to the west. Together they generated so much activity that the capital grew and developed rapidly.

By the late 1950s Addis Ababa was recognized as the unofficial capital of Africa, and thus was made the headquarters of the United Nations Economic Commission for Africa (ECA) in 1958 and later, in 1963, chosen as headquarters of the Organization of African Unity (OAU).

Today Addis Ababa, which bears the imprint of many of these past developments, is a major metropolis, with an estimated population approaching five million.

Located at the centre of Shewa region, the city stands at the very heart of Ethiopia and enjoys excellent connections with all of the country's economic zones. Addis Ababa is Africa's unchallenged diplomatic capital, with more than seventy embassies and consular representatives clustered in the mountain city.

Historian Conti-Rossini once characterized Ethiopia as a 'rich cultural mosaic'. He could also have been speaking about Addis Ababa itself. Each of the country's multitude of ethnic groups is represented somewhere in the capital, as are a large number of foreign residents from all parts of the world who contribute to the city's cosmopolitan atmosphere.

There is much to do and see within the capital, whether at night — at the variety of nightclubs offering all manner of music from

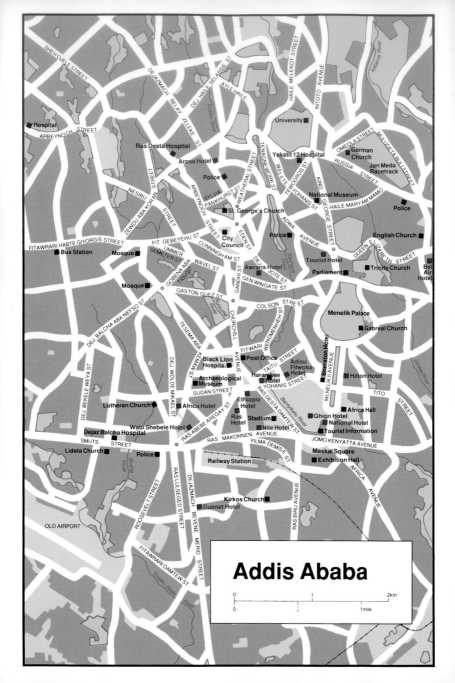

Addis Ababa

0 1 2km

0 1mile

Top: Africa Hall, housing the United Nations Economic Commission for Africa (ECA), features a spectacular stained-glass window by Ethiopian artist Afewerk Tekle.

Above left: A woman sells traditional clothing at the colourful Mercato, the largest market in eastern Africa between Cairo and Johannesburg. Those ready to bargain can find everything from daily Ethiopian necessities to a wide selection of handicrafts and curios.

Above: The Trinity, or Selassie, Cathedral, is one of the most magnificent churches in Addis Ababa and is one of the city's landmarks.

traditional Ethiopian to modern pop, as well as dancing — or by day. The sports-minded will probably already know of the country's global reputation for producing first-class long distance runners, several of whom are world record holders. But those not anxious to try out their running shoes at this high altitude can still take advantage of the tennis — as well as open-air swimming in warm thermal water — offered by several top hotels. In addition, the Addis Ababa stadium offers frequent inter-African and other international as well as local football matches; and there are plenty of opportunities for horse-riding, bowls, and other sports.

Addis Ababa also has a flourishing cultural life. Lectures on such subjects as Ethiopian history and culture are given almost weekly at several locations, and there are frequent exhibitions of Ethiopian art at various galleries in the city.

There are many opportunities to experience Ethiopian music, singing, dance, and theatre. Cultural shows include those given on weekends and holidays at the Hager Fiker Theatre, the National Theatre, City Hall, the Ambassador Theatre, and the Ras Theatre — as well as on weekday evenings at several local hotels and restaurants.

Addis Ababa's cultural *mélange* has resulted in a delicious assortment of restaurants. A wide range of European food (French, Italian, and Greek) is available, as well as Arab, Indian, and Chinese delicacies — not to mention unforgettably tasty Ethiopian cuisine.

The national language, Amharic — Africa's only written language with its own unique script — is widely spoken throughout the country and is predominant in Addis Ababa. The principal foreign languages are English, French, Italian, and Arabic.

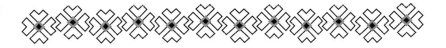

The city is essentially divided into three main sections. To the east lies what may be termed the 'government and educational sector', where — running roughly from north to south — the university, the National Museum, the old Menelik palace, the Hilton Hotel, the Jubilee Palace, and Meskal (Revolution) Square are located.

The central sector is devoted largely to commerce but also houses some government businesses. This runs from Saint George's Cathedral and City Hall in the north to the railway station in the south — all by way of Churchill Road. Here too is the headquarters of the National and Commercial Banks; the main town sales office of Ethiopian Airlines; the Post, Telephone, and Telegraph Office; the main hospital; and the National Theatre.

Also much involved in trade is the western sector, where the famous and colourful Mercato — the largest market in eastern Africa between Cairo and Johannesburg — can be found, as well as the city's main mosque. The south-western sector, which developed later than the centre, is partly residential and partly industrial. It also houses an art museum displaying the works of Ethiopia's premier artist, Afewerk Tekle.

The south-west and south-east are also home to the majority of the embassies, clustered around the roads leading into the city from both the old (Lideta) and the new (Bole) airports.

Happily, the majority of Addis Ababa's principal thoroughfares are wide, two- or four-lane avenues, with trees on both sides and grass reservations in the centre. Many tourist attractions and important offices are found along the capital's main roads, making exploring the city by car easy and enjoyable.

But perhaps the best way to explore Addis is on foot, which allows you to take in much more of the local 'flavour' and see some sights you would perhaps miss if you were in a vehicle.

Many interesting 'day trips' are possible from the capital, such as to some of the beautiful crater lakes in the area (for instance, the lake on top of Mount Zuqualla, Lake Wonchi, or the crater lakes near Debre Zeit); the hot mineral water pools and springs at Sodere, Ambo, or Weliso; or the Blue Nile Gorge (see 'The Blue Nile', p. 52). Day trips that can provide a taste of ancient Ethiopia include those to the Adadi Maryam church (the southernmost stone church similar to those at Lalibela) or to the prehistoric monoliths or stelae at Tiya (see 'An Ancient Land', p. 20).

Opposite: A large, modern, stone stylized Lion of Judah dominates Unity Square near the National Theatre.

Below: Saint George's Cathedral, one of Addis Ababa's fine Ethiopian Orthodox churches, where Haile Selassie was crowned emperor.

An Ancient Land

Ethiopia is old beyond imagination. More than three million years ago, one of our first ancestors walked that portion of the earth that is now Ethiopia: namely, Lucy (*Dinkenesh* to Ethiopians), meaning 'Thou Art Wonderful'. The remains of this 'first human' — an almost complete hominid skeleton — were discovered in 1974 at Hadar on the lower Awash River in Ethiopia's barren and forbidding Danakil region.

It is widely thought that *Dinkenesh's* homeland — Ethiopia — holds the key to a myriad of other questions that have puzzled palaeoanthropologists about our past. To this end, palaeoanthropological and archaeological work continues at Hadar and at a number of other sites along the Ethiopia section of the Great Rift Valley and in the Omo Valley.

These often bleak, sparsely inhabited regions have already yielded some fine examples of Stone Age tools from deposits up to 1.7 million years old, and remains of *Homo erectus* from deposits some 800,000 years old.

One of these sites, Melka Konture, is relatively close to Addis Ababa. Since 1965, geologists and archaeologists have had a compound there, some 60 kilometres south of the capital on the Addis–Butajira road, set up to excavate that which the earliest humans left behind. Many examples of beautiful two-edged hand-axes, obsidian scrapers, and sets of 'bolas' — the round stones used several together in nets to throw at animals — have been found. Fossilized bones of hippopotamus, rhinoceros, elephant, and antelope have also been unearthed here.

But early man was as much an artist as a toolmaker: some fine, delicate paintings have been discovered on cave walls — such as at

Porc Epic near Dire Dawa and Dilla, about 300 kilometres south of Addis Ababa — estimated at 400,000 years old.

Not as ancient, but equally fascinating relics of the past are the crudely fashioned stone 'monuments' — often referred to as monoliths or stelae — found at Dilla and Tiya, a small village about forty kilometres south of Melka Konture. The Tiya location, whose monuments have markings believed to date from about 1300–1500 AD, has been proclaimed a World Heritage Site.

But perhaps the world's most famous and mysterious stelae still stand silent sentry in Ethiopia's northern regions, in Aum, once reputed to be the home of the legendary Queen of Sheba.

Although its very early history is still unknown, Ethiopian legends, first recorded in the fourteenth-century *Kebre Nagast* (Book of Kings), proclaim Axum as Sheba's tenth-century BC capital. It seems certain that a high civilization was established here by immigrants from southern Arabia before the Christian era, and that by the first century AD — the time of the earliest historical records — Axum was well known to Greek traders as a fine city and the centre of a very considerable empire.

Rising to importance around the time of the birth of Christ, Axum was the capital of the far-reaching Axumite kingdom — a kingdom that dominated the vital crossroads between Africa and Asia for almost a thousand years — and the location of its principal ecclesiastical building: the Church of St Mary of Zion, where, according to legend, the biblical Ark of the Covenant was placed. The Axumites introduced a written language, Ge'ez, and created a new imperial power and political cohesion. They also gave Ethiopia its first organized religion — Christianity —

Below: Many important archaeological finds have been made — and continue to be made — in Ethiopia, helping palaeoanthropologists fill in many of the missing pieces of the puzzle of our past.

Opposite: Crudely fashioned stone monoliths, which some believe to be ancient grave markers, abound in Tiya, a World Heritage Site.

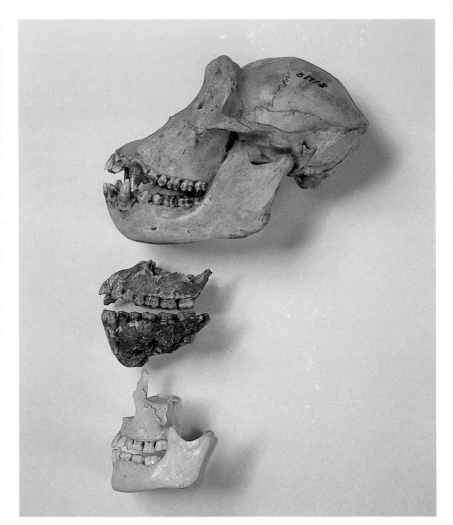

in the fourth century AD.

The spectacular rise of Islam in the seventh century was the main cause of Axum's decline. Although there was no direct aggression, Arab influence in the Red Sea cut off trade and cultural relations, and Ethiopia found itself isolated from the rest of the world.

However, even after the realm's decline, the city remained Ethiopia's religious capital as well as the place where several medieval emperors went to be officially crowned. The town abounds in archaeological remains — including the graves of kings, the foundations of a palace, inscribed tablets, and great carved obelisks.

It is with these famous obelisks, or monolithic stelae, that Axum is widely identified. In ancient times, seven of these monoliths of granite stood together; but the biggest, the largest monolith ever made anywhere in the world — measuring over thirty-three metres (108 feet) and weighing about 500 tons — fell at some remote period in the past and now lies smashed on the ground to the right of the standing stele. The second-largest stele, about twenty-four metres (79 feet) high, also fell and was stolen during the Fascist Italian occupation on the personal orders of the dictator Mussolini. It remains in Rome, where it was taken in 1937. However, the third-largest stele, measuring twenty-three metres (75 feet), still stands in Axum.

All seven giant stelae are made of single pieces of granite and have identical decoration. Each resembles a tall, slender multi-storeyed house in the architectural style of the Axumite houses and palaces and is decorated with representations of doors, windows, and, in some cases, door handles.

Also of great interest is Axum's Church of Saint Mary of Zion. There are, in fact, two such churches, one old and one new, both located in a spacious walled compound directly opposite the Park of the Stelae. The older, a rectangular battlemented building, was put up in the early seventeenth century by Emperor Fasilidas; the modern structure was erected nearby by Emperor Haile Selassie, who opened it in the company of England's Queen Elizabeth II in 1965. The older structure, by far the more interesting, is the repository of many royal crowns and other valuables. Unfortunately, it is closed to women, who are, however, allowed to inspect some of these treasures, which are carried to the edge of the church precincts for this purpose. The church courtyard also contains many antiquities, including sculpted stones, which obviously formed part of the earlier church. Visitors may also see the stone thrones on which the monarchs of the past were crowned, as well as other stone chairs reserved for bishops and courtiers.

Nearby are the ruins of the original church, which, according to tradition, was erected soon after the state adopted Christianity as its religion in the early fourth century.

Perhaps the greatest mystery about this strange, ancient city is the claim that it is the last resting place of the Ark of the Covenant — a claim connected in Ethiopian tradition to the Queen of Sheba and King Solomon, whose son Menelik is said to have brought the Ark to Axum 3,000 years ago and to have founded the Solomonic dynasty, of which Haile Selassie was the last emperor. The well guarded sanctuary chapel of the Ark of the Covenant stands in the town — which the visitor may approach but never hope to enter.

There are a number of sites associated by local folk with the

Left: Mysterious giant stelae still stand in Axum in northern Ethiopia, silent testimony to the ancient and powerful Axumite kingdom.

Below: The crown of Menelik II, one of many treasures housed in Axum's Church of Saint Mary of Zion.

Queen of Sheba herself. The most notable is a huge water reservoir, hewn out of solid rock, known as the Queen of Sheba's Bath. It is the focal point of the annual ceremony of *Timkat* (Epiphany) in which, each January, a replica of the Ark is carried in procession.

Almost equally impressive are the ruins of the so-called Queen of Sheba's Palace — a great and well-built edifice with finely mortared stone walls, deep foundations and an impressive drainage system, which stands on the outskirts of town on the Gondar road.

Across the road, in a field facing the palace, visitors may also inspect a number of rough-hewn granite stelae, some standing more than four metres (13 feet) high, some fallen and broken. Most are undecorated but one, the largest, is carved with four horizontal bands, each topped by a row of circles in relief. This crude obelisk, much older than those in the Park of the Stelae, is thought by the townspeople to mark the Queen of Sheba's grave.

Axum is but one stop on Ethiopia's famed Historic Route, a well trodden path through the country's best known historic places of interest, easy to see because all are regular daily stops on Ethiopian Airlines' domestic route.

But the visitor who has a little more time should veer off the beaten track — particularly in the fascinating Tigray region — to discover some of the country's most amazing historical treasures.

For example, Ethiopia's earliest known capital, Yeha, lies in a remote part of the region several hours' drive from Axum through some dramatic highland scenery. But, as the birthplace of the country's earliest high civilization, it is well worth visiting. There are the imposing ruins of Yeha's Temple of the Moon — a large,

pre-Christian shrine erected around the fifth century BC — as well as a modern church dedicated to Abba Aftse, one of the 'Nine Saints' from Syria who founded many important monasteries in northern Ethiopia in the fifth and sixth centuries. The building's front façade has been fitted with stones from the original temple, and the church contains many crosses, old manuscripts, and stones bearing ancient Sabaean inscriptions, all of which can be seen on request.

Another 'hidden treasure' lies on a distinctive flat-topped mountain in the same region: the ancient monastery of Debre Damo — difficult to reach, but most rewarding for any man (women are not allowed in) determined enough to visit it.

The monastery, which dates back to early Axumite times, is said to possess the Ethiopia's oldest existing church. Legend has it that Abba Aragawi, one of the 'Nine Saints', while wandering at the foot of the cliff, judged that the plateau above him was a suitable place to live a solitary life. God, hearing his wish, commanded a snake living on the mountain-top to stretch down and lift up the holy man, who made Debre Damo his abode.

The visitor, lacking the kind snake that helped the monastery's founder to ascend the mountain, has to go up using a rope lowered by the friendly monks. The summit, when eventually conquered twenty-four metres (78 feet) later, offers panoramic views and complete seclusion and peace for the 100 or so monks and deacons who live there.

The beams and ceiling of the ancient Debre Damo church — around which the monastery is built — are beautifully decorated with carved wooden panels depicting lion, elephant, rhinoceros,

Below: Access to the remote Debre Damo monastery is only gained by climbing a rope (far right of picture) up a steep cliffside.

Opposite: Solitary priest outside another of Tigray's fascinating rock-hewn churches, Endo Medhane Alem.

Opposite left: Priests display ancient ceremonial fan outside Debra Tsion church.

Opposite right: Many of Tigray's churches are adorned with beautiful murals, such as this one in the Abune Yemata church.

31

snakes, gazelle, antelope, giraffe, and camels. A large number of paintings are preserved there, including several depicting Abba Aragawi's legendary foundation of Debre Damo.

The treasures secreted within — kept intact through the monastery's 1,400 tumultuous years of history because of that arduous, dangerous ascent — include an extensive collection of illuminated manuscripts, among them the oldest surviving text fragments anywhere in Ethiopia. The church now houses about fifty manuscripts, although the monks claim they once possessed no less than a thousand.

Further south of Debra Damo lies the regional capital of Makale, from where the adventurous can make arrangements to visit the more than 130 known rock-hewn churches scattered over the mountains of Tigray. They vary from modified caves, very crudely enlarged and shaped, to highly sophisticated, finely hewn structures, cut into the rocky cliffs with consummate skill and patience. Some churches have been elaborately decorated with paintings and carvings on walls, ceilings, and pillars.

Experts disagree as to the age, origin, and development of these churches, but it is thought that this unique form of church building in the region developed during the latter half of the Axumite empire. Places of worship were excavated from rocky cliffs, many hewn in extremely inaccessible spots with secluded entrances — possibly as a form of defense.

Most of the old churches are still in active use today and have been through the intervening centuries. They have been the guardians of religious life and culture through aeons of turmoil and change, and remain some of the priceless wonders of Ethiopia.

Overleaf: The remarkable church of Bet Giyorgis, often considered the most elegant of all the Lalibela structures.

But what has become known as the 'Eighth Wonder of the World' lies further south, on a natural 2,600-metre (8,500-foot) rock terrace surrounded on all sides by rugged and forbidding mountains in the northern extreme of Wollo region: the marvellous monastic settlement of Lalibela.

Formerly known as Roha, Lalibela now bears the name of King Lalibela (1181-1221), a member of the Zagwe dynasty. Shortly after his birth at Roha, the future king's mystical life began to unfold. Legend has it that one day his mother saw him lying happily in his cradle surrounded by a dense swarm of bees. Recalling an old Ethiopian belief that the animal world could foretell the advent of important personages, the second sight came upon her and she cried out: 'The bees know that this child will become King.' Accordingly, she called her son 'Lalibela', which means 'the bee recognizes his sovereignty'.

Lalibela's older brother, Harbay, the incumbent monarch, was naturally disturbed to hear this news and unsuccessfully tried to have his brother murdered. Persecution continued for several years, culminating in a deadly potion that left the young prince in mortal sleep. During the three-day stupor, Lalibela was transported by angels to heaven, where God ordered him to return to Roha and build churches the like of which the world had never seen before. The Almighty, it is said, also told the prince how to design those churches, where to build them, and how to decorate them.

After Lalibela resumed mortal existence, Harbay — acting on God's instructions — went to pay homage to Lalibela and beg his forgiveness. The two brothers then rode together on the same mule to Roha, and Harbay abdicated in favour of his younger brother.

33

When Lalibela was crowned, he gathered masons, carpenters, tools, set down a wage scale, and purchased the land needed for building. The churches went up with extraordinary speed, goes the legend, because the angels continued the work at night.

Those who scoff at the tale are soon silenced when they glimpse the famous Lalibela churches. Physically prised from the rock on which they stand, these towering edifices seem superhuman in scale, workmanship, and concept. Some lie almost completely hidden in deep trenches, while others stand in open quarried caves. A complex and bewildering labyrinth of tunnels and narrow passageways with offset crypts, grottos, and galleries connects them all. Throughout this mysterious and wonderful settlement, priests and deacons go about their timeless business.

Seeing all of the Lalibela churches takes a long time, but they are well worth the visitor's effort — particularly during the colourful Ethiopian Christmas and *Timkat* (Epiphany) celebrations (on January 7th and January 19th respectively).

The churches can be divided into two main groups.

The first group of six lies in rock cradles one behind the other north of a stream known locally as the Jordan River: Bet Golgotha, Bet Mika'el (also known as Bet Debre Sina), Bet Maryam, Bet Meskel, Bet Danaghel, and Bet Medhane Alem.

Bet Medhane Alem is the largest of all the Lalibela churches. Built like a Greek temple, it is unusual, being entirely surrounded by square columns, with a further forest of twenty-eight massive rectangular columns supporting the roof inside. Polished by centuries of pressure from countless feet, the stone

floor reflects shafts of light from apertures in the walls high above. In a corner, one can see three empty graves said to have been symbolically dug for biblical patriarchs Abraham, Isaac, and Jacob.

The interconnected churches of Bet Golgotha and Bet Mika'el form the most mysterious complex in Lalibela. Its holiest shrine — the Selassie Chapel — is housed here, and, according to the whispers of the priests, perhaps even the tomb of King Lalibela himself. Some of the most beautiful processional crosses of Lalibela are here. One, a very rich and elaborate metal cross, black with age and decorated with inlaid circles, is said to have belonged to Lalibela.

Also to the north of the Jordan, but much further to the west, and somewhat isolated from the others, is the remarkable church of Bet Giyorgis, possibly the most elegant of all the Lalibela structures, located in the south-west of the village on a sloping rock terrace. In a deep pit with perpendicular walls, it can only be reached through a tunnel entered a distance away through a trench. Small round caves and chambers have been found in the courtyard walls — graves for pious pilgrims and monks.

Legend says that when King Lalibela had almost completed his churches, he was severely reproached by Ethiopia's 'national saint', Saint George — who in full armour rode up to him on his white horse — for not having constructed a house for him. Lalibela thereupon promised the saint the most beautiful church, and Saint George apparently personally supervised the work, as attested to by the fact that the monks still show the hoof marks

Opposite: Seemingly oblivious to visitors, Lalibela's monks lead a solitary and pious existence.

Right: Young boy outside another of the region's remarkable churches, Gennata Maryam.

Right: Not far from Lalibela are a number of other fascinating rock-hewn churches, including Na'akuto La'ab, which is built in a cave.

Opposite: Monk precariously crosses into the rook of Lalibela's Bet Amanuel.

of his horse to visitors today.

Standing on a three-tiered plinth, Bet Giyorgis is shaped like a Greek cross and has walls — with an alternation of projecting and recessing horizontal layers — reminiscent of Axumite architecture. The church also has an elaborately shaped doorway.

The group south of the Jordan River comprises four churches: Bet Emanuel, Bet Mercurios, Bet Abba Libanos, and Bet Gabriel-Rufa'el.

Bet Emanuel is perhaps the finest; its elaborate exterior much praised by art historians. The structure contains a large hall with four pillars, and its irregularly placed windows are Axumite in style, as are the walls. A spiral staircase leads up to an upper storey. The most striking interior feature is the double frieze of blind windows in the vaulted nave, the lower frieze being purely ornamental and the upper consisting of windows (to provide light from the galleries) alternating with decorated areas.

Chambers and cavities for sacred bees in the outer wall of the courtyard are a reminder of the bees that prophesied kingship to Lalibela. Some of the chambers, however, are the graves of monks and pilgrims who wanted to be buried in this 'holy city'.

Although not as famous as those in Lalibela, not far away (a worthwhile trek over the Lalibela Mountains), are the equally fascinating rock-hewn churches of Ashetan Maryam, Na'akuto La'ab, and Yemrehanna Krestos.

More than mere monuments, the churches in and around Lalibela are a living link with the past and testify to the power and spirit of an ancient Christian faith.

From kings and churches to emperors and castles: another not-to-be-missed stop on Ethiopia's Historic Route is what has been called the 'Camelot' of Africa: Gondar.

It is easy to imagine the intrigue and pageantry that took place back in the seventeenth and eighteenth centuries, when Gondar, then the Ethiopian capital, was home to a number of emperors and warlords, courtiers and kings. One only has to stroll through the banqueting halls and gaze down from the balconies of the many castles and palaces here to drift back into a long-ago world of battles and court conspiracies.

Nestled in the foothills of the Simien Mountains in north-western Ethiopia, Gondar became the capital during the reign of Emperor Fasilidas (1632-1667), who built the first of a number of castle-like palaces to be found here. He established a tradition that was followed by most of his successors, whose buildings greatly enhanced the city's grandeur.

Gondar, which rose to prominence after Ethiopia went through a long period without a fixed capital, emerged in the seventeenth century as the country's largest settlement. In its day, the city was an important administrative, commercial, religious, and cultural centre. It was famous for its sophisticated aristocratic life, its church scholarship, and its extensive trade, which took its merchants to Sudan and the port of Massawa as well as to the rich lands south of the Blue Nile. Gondar was also noted for the skill of its many craftsmen.

The city retained its pre-eminence until the middle of the nineteenth century, when Emperor Tewodros II moved his seat of government to Debre Tabor and later to Mekdela. As a result,

Opposite: Gondar, the 'Camelot' of Africa, features a number of castle-like palaces, such as this one of Emperor Fasilidas.

Below: The devoted surround 'Fasilidas' Bath', a 'bathing palace' filled with water once a year for the Timkat *celebrations.*

Gondar declined greatly in importance and was subsequently looted in the 1880s by the Sudanese Dervishes. By the early nineteenth century the city was a mere shadow of its former self. More recently, its appearance was not aided by the fact that several historic buildings were damaged by British bombs during Ethiopia's liberation campaign of 1941. Most of Gondar's famous castles and other imperial buildings nevertheless survived the ravages of time and together constitute one of Ethiopia's most fascinating antiquities.

The oldest and most impressive of Gondar's imperial structures is the two-storeyed palace of Emperor Fasilidas, built of roughly hewn brown basalt stones held together with mortar. Said to have been the work of an Indian architect, the building has a flat roof, a rectangular tower in the south-west corner — which affords a distant view of Lake Tana — four smaller domed towers, and a battlemented parapet.

Other buildings in the 'imperial quarter' include the library of Fasilidas's son, Emperor Yohannes I (1667-1682), a cube-like two-storeyed structure with an outside staircase and a parapeted flat roof; a nearby chancellery with a slender square tower and another outside staircase; the saddle-shaped castle of Yohannes' son, Emperor Iyasu I (1682-1706), with a small conical tower and spiralled outer staircase; the large hall, or 'house of song', of Emperor Dawit II (1716-1721), in which many ceremonies once took place; the long V-shaped reception and banqueting hall of Emperor Bakaffa (1722-1730); and the great two-storeyed palace, charmingly decorated with Ethiopian crosses in mauve-coloured tuff, of the latter's redoubtable consort Empress

Mentewab. The palace compound is also the site of the grave of one the most remarkable nineteenth-century foreign travellers to Ethiopia: Emperor Tewodros's close friend Walter Plowden, a sometime British consul.

In addition to the fine structures in the imperial compound, visitors should see the palace of Ras Mika'el Sehul and the house of the *Echege*. The former, a small structure modelled on the Fasilidas castle, owes its name to its most important occupant, who became Gondar's dictator during the monarchy's decline in the eighteenth century. The latter building is a round structure once inhabited by the *Echege*, the second most important official of the Ethiopian church. This little-known building is located in one of the humbler parts of the town and is known to many only by its urban registration number: House No. 1, Kebele 11. It can be reached by a short but interesting walk through town.

Several notable Gondarine structures are to be seen outside town. The most impressive, located in the Kaha River valley south of Gondar, is a well-preserved 'bathing palace' variously attributed to Fasilidas or Iyasu I. It stands in a rectangular, neatly walled depression, which is filled with water once a year for the *Timkat*, or Epiphany, celebrations, and, though popularly referred to as a 'bathing palace', was probably constructed for such celebrations.

Rulers of this era also developed the area in the hills north-west of the town — called Kweskwam after the home of the Virgin Mary — as a kind of 'Capitol Hill' for government buildings. Most are now ruins, including the largest — a square, three-storeyed castle with a flat parapet roof and battlemented walls, embellished with a series of bas–reliefs of various Ethiopian animals. Visitors to the

church here can, on request, see many fine old Gondarine manuscripts, and enter a crypt containing the skeletal remains of the famous eighteenth-century Empress Mentewab, her son Emperor Iyasu II, and grandson Emperor Iyo'as.

Gondar was the site of numerous fine churches, a number of which have survived to this day. Perhaps the finest of the Gondarine churches is that of Debre Birhan Selassie or 'Light of the Trinity', which stands on raised ground about a half an hour's walk to the north-east. An imposing rectangular structure, its ceilings are decorated with beautiful winged angels and its walls with impressive scenes depicting biblical events, including the lives of Christ, Mary, the saints and the martyrs.

Offering startling contrast to the churches and castles of Ethiopian's Christian history, the romantic walled city of Harar provides a glimpse into the country's equally fascinating Islamic past.

Harar, the capital of the Harerge region, came into formal existence in 1520 when a local amir, Abu Bekr Mahomed, moved his capital there from Dakar, site of an older nearby settlement. His rule, however, was soon cut short, for he was murdered five years later by Ahmed Gragn, or Ahmed the Left-Handed. Gragn left his homeland in 1530-31 to begin a *jihad*, or holy war, against the Christian Ethiopian empire. He overran much of it, but, as a result of Portuguese intervention, was defeated and killed in 1543.

The city, impoverished by war, faced many difficulties. The Oromo advanced into the surrounding countryside. This isolated Harar and caused Gragn's nephew and successor, Nur ibn al-Wazir Mujahid, to erect strong encircling walls, which ever since that time have been one of the city's most dominant features.

Harar also was — and still is — well known for its Islamic learning and scholarship, as well as its handicrafts, including weaving, basket-making, and book binding. Harar is also famed for its silversmiths.

A bright splash of colour is provided by the Harari women strolling through town, often dressed in red, purple, or black dresses with velvet trousers and bright orange shawls and balancing heavy bundles of cloth or baskets on their heads.

Places of interest inside the city include the impressive centuries-old walls themselves, which had five gates until 1889, when the Ethiopians built two more: the Gate of the Duke and the Berbera Gate. The latter was closed by the Italians, but the former is where the main street enters into the old city.

Also of interest is Ras Makonnen's stately old palace and the Jami Mosque, which dates back to the seventeenth century. The mosque's slender minaret, however was built in 1761-62. Women are not allowed to enter and photography is not permitted.

Near the mosque is the fine, large Rimbaud House — said (incorrectly) to have once been occupied by the famous French poet of that name.

On the north side of the town's interesting Muslim Market is a small, white mosque-like structure, the tomb of Abu Said Ali, an early Muslim religious leader of the town. Beneath his tomb is said to be a well which can provide water for the entire town in case of siege.

From the remains of the first humans to amazing manifestations of religious allegiance, Ethiopia is truly a country with an unforgettable 'living past'.

The Blue Nile

The mysterious Nile was long hidden from Western geographers and explorers. It was not until the expeditions of such great travellers as Bruce, Burton, and Speke that the secret of this grand river — which had fascinated, and eluded, even the ancient Romans and Greeks — was revealed. It was then confirmed that the White Nile originates in East Africa's Lake Victoria, while the Blue Nile pours out of Ethiopia's Lake Tana. The two rivers merge into the Nile proper at Khartoum, the Sudanese capital.

As it plunges more than 2,000 metres (6,560 feet) in its 800-kilometre (497-mile) course from Ethiopia to the Sudanese plains, the Blue Nile is what embodies the drama and mystery of the great river of history — beginning its journey with a thundering cascade over the exceptional Blue Nile Falls, thirty kilometres (19 miles) downstream from the point where it leaves Lake Tana.

Known locally as *Tis Isat* — 'Smoke of Fire' — the Blue Nile Falls are the most dramatic spectacle that the whole Nile system has to offer. Four hundred metres (1,312 feet) wide when in flood (which normally occurs in September and October, after the rainy season), and dropping over a sheer chasm more than forty-five metres (150 feet) deep, the falls throw up a continuous spray of water droplets which drench onlookers up to a kilometre away. This misty deluge, in turn, produces rainbows that shift and shimmer across the gorge and a perennial rainforest of lush green vegetation — much to the delight of the innumerable monkeys and multi-coloured birds that inhabit the gorge.

It is only a five-minute drive from the lakeside town of Bahar Dar, across the Blue Nile Bridge, to the spot where the famous river flows out of Lake Tana. But the falls are about thirty-five kilometres (22

miles) south of the town and are best approached from Tis Isat village, a market settlement of the Amhara people who live in this area farming crops like wheat, sorghum and *teff* (from which *injera*, the national bread, is made).

On leaving the village the footpath meanders first beside fertile open fields, then drops into a deep basaltic rift spanned by an ancient, fortified stone bridge built in the seventeenth century by Portuguese adventurers and still in use. After about a thirty-minute walk, a stiff climb up a grassy hillside is then rewarded by a magnificent view of the falls, breaking the smooth edge of the rolling river into a thundering cataract of foaming white water.

The site overlooking the waterfall has been visited over the years by many notable visitors, including the late eighteenth-century Scottish traveller James Bruce, and, in more recent times, Britain's Queen Elizabeth II.

Although not so spectacular, the Blue Nile Gorge near the falls — often providing views reminiscent of America's Grand Canyon — also has breathtaking scenery. Other impressive gorges are formed by various tributaries of the Nile, such as the one near Debre Tsige, which is about sixty-nine kilometres (43 miles) from Addis Ababa. Thirteen kilometres (eight miles) further on, a sheer cliff drops more than 1,000 metres (3,000 feet) into another awesome gorge, formed by the Zega Wodel River, one of the Blue Nile tributaries.

Ancient Monasteries
Nearby is the Debre Libanos monastery, perched beneath a cliff on

Opposite: The legendary Blue Nile River cuts a path through much of Ethiopia, creating some spectacular gorges.

Opposite bottom: Near the Blue Nile Falls is an ancient bridge built in the 17th century by Portuguese explorers.

Below: Known locally as Tis Isat, *or 'Smoke of Fire', the dramatic Blue Nile Falls throw up a continuous mist that can be felt up to a kilometre away.*

the edge of a gorge, overlooking the river. The original monastic buildings have long since disappeared — destroyed, it is said, during the wars of Ahmed Gragn. They were replaced by a succession of structures, the latest a spectacular modern church erected after World War II on Emperor Haile Selassie's orders. In addition to the intricate mosaic figures on the façade, the church has beautiful stained glass windows and contains some interesting mural paintings by well-known Ethiopian artist Afewerk Tekle. To the left of the church is the nuns' residence, built in the 1920s, and to the right, behind the church, a cave containing holy water. Nearby are the huge monks' kitchens, dating from the early 20th century.

The monastic establishment was founded in the thirteenth century by Tekle Haymanot, one of the Ethiopian Orthodox Church's most renowned saints. According to legend he was so holy that for seven years he prayed standing on one leg, with the result that the other fell off. Many traditional Ethiopian religious paintings depict him in that condition.

The monastery was particularly important during the reign of Emperor Menelik, who travelled there during his last fatal illness to sample its reputedly curative holy waters. Many noblemen and others also went there on pilgrimage, and not a few important figures are buried in the precincts. Later, in 1937, during the Italian occupation, the Debre Libanos monks incurred the wrath of the Fascist viceroy Graziani, who ordered their execution, 'all without distinction'; 297 monks were shot, after which he proudly reported that 'of Debre Libanos there remains no more trace'. The martyrs' bones can still be seen at the monastery.

One should also see the House of the Cross, which is decorated internally with interesting paintings, and said to house a cross that belonged to Tekle Haymanot; the monks' kitchens, accessible only to men; and, nearby, those of the nuns, open to all visitors.

A hundred metres beyond the monastery turnoff, a five-minute walk right towards the gorge brings one to a bridge from which there is a fine view of the countryside far below. This bridge is popularly described as sixteenth-century Portuguese but was, in fact, built in the late nineteenth century by an Ethiopian nobleman, Emperor Menelik's uncle Ras Darge. It is possible to climb down below the bridge to where some waterfalls start their 600-metre (2,000-foot) plunge to the abyss below, or walk along the cliff edge to look back at the falls and the bridge.

Rivalling the attraction of the Blue Nile Falls are the thirty-seven islands scattered about on the 3,000-square-kilometre (1,860-square-mile) surface of Ethiopia's largest body of water: Lake Tana, which gives birth to the Blue Nile. Some twenty of these shelter churches and monasteries of immense historical and cultural interest; decorated with beautiful paintings and housing innumerable treasures.

The islands and peninsulas of Lake Tana are most conveniently approached by boat from Bahar Dar on the southern side of the lake, though boats can often also be obtained at Gorgora on the northern shore.

The many interesting and historic locations on or around the lake include the islands of Birgida Maryam, Dega Estefanos, Dek, Narga, Tana Cherkos, Mitsele Fasilidas, Kebran, and Debre

Above: Lake Tana's island monasteries house a myriad of treasures and beautiful paintings.

Left: Although they look extremely precarious, the tankwas *that ply the waters of Lake Tana are actually amazingly sturdy.*

Opposite: Ruins of the castle of Emperor Susneyos stand on a precipice overlooking Lake Tana.

Maryam, as well as the Gorgora, Mandaba, and Zeghe peninsulas. All have fine churches. Though founded much earlier, most of the actual buildings date from the late sixteenth or early seventeenth centuries. Many have beautiful mural paintings and church crosses, and house crowns and clothes of former kings.

Access to the churches is, for the most part, closed to women; they are allowed to land on the banks of the islands but not permitted to proceed any further. The clergy sometimes agree to bring some of their treasures to the water's edge for women visitors to inspect.

Women are, however, permitted to visit churches on the Zeghe peninsula, the nearby church of Ura Kidane Mehret, and Narga Selassie.

Kebran Gabriel, the nearest monastery to Bahar Dar, is a principal tourist attraction. Established in the fourteenth century and rebuilt during the reign of Emperor Iyasu I (1682-1706), it is an unassuming but nevertheless impressive building with a distinct cathedral atmosphere.

Ura Kidane Mehret is another popular attraction, with the added advantage that women are allowed inside. Located on the Zeghe peninsula, the monastery is an integral part of the local community. The church design dates from the same time as that of the Kebran Gabriel church, but it is a more decorative building, with colourful frescoes depicting biblical scenes from biblical lore and the history of the Ethiopian Orthodox Church.

The third principal attraction is Dega Estefanos, which is also closed to women. Although farther away from Bahar Dar, it is well worth visiting. A steep trek up a winding path leads towards the

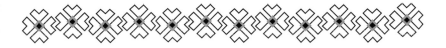

monastery on the summit. Some ninety metres (300 feet) above the lake's surface are low, round, thatched-roof buildings that house the monks, and nearby an arch set into a high stone wall leads to a grassy clearing, at the centre of which stands the church of St Stephanos, a relatively new building erected about a century ago after the original structure had burned down in a grass fire.

The real historic interest in Dega Estefanos, however, lies in its treasury. Here, together with numerous piles of brightly coloured ceremonial robes, are coffins containing the mummified remains of several former emperors: Yekuno Amlak, who restored the Solomonic dynasty in 1270; Dawit, late fourteenth century; Zara Yaqob, fifteenth century; Za Dengel, early seventeenth century; and Fasilidas, also seventeenth century. The modern, glass-sided coffins allow visitors to view the mummified bodies.

Dega Estefanos is also said to have served as a temporary hiding place for Ethiopia's most jealously guarded religious relic — the Ark of the Covenant. Tradition has it that the Ark was brought to the island for safekeeping in the sixteenth century, when the Muslim forces of warlord Ahmed Gragn attacked and occupied Axum, where the Ark normally rested.

History aside, bird lovers should make a point to visit Fasilidas Island, near the eastern side of the lake. And, of course, when moving around on the lake, be sure to notice the interesting *tankwa* boats, which may be seen making their way between the islands and the mainland. These little papyrus boats, open at the back end, appear dangerously unwaterworthy as they slide over the surface, but they continue to carry passengers and goods to and from the islands as they have done for centuries.

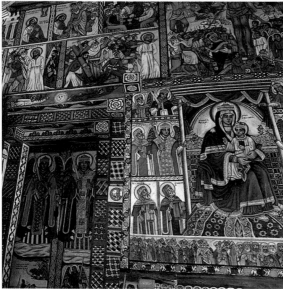

Above: As they have done for centuries, men build tankwas *on the shores of Lake Tana.*

Left: Intricate murals adorn the walls of Mandaba Island's Amde Tsion monastery.

Opposite: Priests stand under the ancient arch of a rare church built by King Ezana, Ethiopia's first Christian monarch.

Mountain Majesties

Ethiopia's geology is based primarily on an old crystalline block, which once also covered an immense area from the Brazilian plateau to India's Deccan. Formed early in the earth's history, this block later cracked after its three component parts — American, African, and Asian — drifted apart. The country's bedrock, therefore, belongs to the earth's first continent, which geologists call Gondwanaland, of which Africa is the largest intact remnant.

The hard crystalline rocks of the African block consist of granites and gneiss, and contain many valuable deposits. Parts of the Ethiopian area were once under the sea, so that there are also many sedimentary rocks, mainly limestones and sandstones, in addition to later volcanic materials found in layers above the old crystalline rocks.

In some places rain has eroded the more recent rocks, exposing the original rocks. Nowhere is this more prominent — and stunning — than in Ethiopia's northern Simien region. This was the epicentre of much volcanic activity about forty million years ago, and the resulting outpouring of a boiling mass of white-hot lava reached a thickness of some 3,000 metres (9,840 feet) in this area before it stopped. Subsequent erosion of this volcanic core has produced the dramatic highs and lows of the Simiens: deep precipices and gorges, tall pinnacles of jagged rock, and weird, withered landscapes.

The region includes many summits above 4,000 metres (13,000 feet), and culminates in the highest point in Ethiopia, Ras Dashen, which, at 4,543 metres (14,901 feet), is also Africa's fourth highest mountain. It is not a difficult mountain to climb and can be reached by travelling through the Simien Mountains National Park.

The base from which to explore the small 179-square-kilometre (111 square-mile) park is Debark, 740 kilometres (464 miles) north-west of Addis Ababa and 101 kilometres (63 miles) north of Gondar.

The first thing any visitor must do is rent pack and riding animals and hire guides for the six-hour trip into the park. Although it helps to inquire in Addis Ababa before you leave concerning dealers and current prices, the hiring of guides, mules, and muleteers is done through the national park headquarters.

As the only 'motorable' dry weather road in the park — up to Sankaber Camp — is not always in good condition, transport of the four-legged variety is by far the more reliable means of getting around.

Suitable clothing for extreme temperatures are needed as the diurnal swing is considerable. Waterproof clothing is also necessary, as are a hat and sunscreen lotion: at these altitudes the sun can burn fiercely. Water is available from the various streams but should be treated. It is wise to remember that the main luggage is loaded on mules for the day, so the day's needs should be carried in a separate pack.

There are various campsites and tracks to follow and it is best to take the advice of the guides. The topography of this park will remain in the mind forever. Climbing up from Debark on mules, through extensive farmland, the visitor is unaware of the dramatic scenery about to unfold. The land forms various small

Below: Giant lobelias reach skyward, breaking up the seemingly barren landscape seen on the trek up to the Simien Mountains.

Right: The craggy pinnacles and crevices of the Simiens.

plateaux, and the edges of these plunge dramatically to the lowlands to the north and east. The gorge edges form a perfect habitat for the animal that the park was set up to protect — the Walia ibex.

Generally the first stop is Sankaber Camp, a trek that leads mainly through cultivated areas to the 3,230-metre (10,600-foot) campsite. From this point, visitors can walk to the edge of the abyss, where they may get their first glimpse of the spectacular scenery. Much of the vegetation has been altered by humans over the years and few trees will be seen in the area except the introduced eucalyptus. But in inaccessible areas, such as the escarpment, natural habitats are preserved and plants such as St. John's wort and heather are seen as small trees or bushes, and many smaller herbs form carpets of colour. Among these are many species of *Alchemilla*, the tall spikes of various 'red-hot pokers', and carpets of small blue lobelia flowers.

Probably the easiest animal to see in this area is the endemic gelada baboon, which grass eaters and will often be seen in family units, one male guarding his harem of females and young ones. They are also known as the 'bleeding heart baboons' from the red areas on the chest that show the sexual state of the animal. The klipspringer may be seen on rocky areas, its hooves specially adapted to leaping from rock to rock. The small grey duiker inhabits any area where there is enough cover to protect it from enemies.

Though named after this area, the Simien fox, also referred to as the Simien jackal or Ethiopian wolf, is now very rare here, with only about thirty animals remaining. They are more com-

mon in Bale Mountains National Park in the south. Its high-pitched call may be heard at night, and its bright red coat is distinctive if seen during the day. It feeds on the many species of rodents found here.

The animal most visitors wish to see is the Walia ibex. This member of the wild goat family has magnificent heavily ridged horns sweeping back over the shoulders. The Walia live on the crags of the steep escarpment, their hooves clinging to the smallest ledge.

The birds here often provide spectacular aerobatic displays off the sheer cliffs, using the air currents peculiar to the terrain. Lammergeyers and choughs are present, as well as endemics such as the thick-billed raven, black-headed siskin, white collared pigeon, wattled ibis, white-billed starling, spot-breasted plover, and white-backed black tit.

From Sankaber, the track leads through meadows, forests, and some cultivated areas to Geech, a three- to three-and-a-half-hour trip by mule. Geech, at 3,660 metres (11,800 feet), is worth a stay of at least two days: there are several good lookout spots where one may see Walia, gelada, and klipspringer, and breath taking views from nearby peaks.

From Geech to the next stopping-off point, Ch'enek, the journey takes another two-and-a-half to four hours, and trekkers may have to dismount and walk part of the way where the climb is steep. The Ch'enek campsite offers superb views, and there are many places to see Walia ibex. There are also caves to explore, and this is the only place in the park where — if extremely lucky — one can see rock hyrax, the small mammal

Below: 'Man of the Mountains': one of the hardy Amhara people who manage to eke out a living in the cold, sometimes harsh, environment of the Simien Mountains.

Right: The 'bleeding heart' and shaggy coat of the endemic gelada baboon are its distinctive characteristics.

that looks like an overgrown guinea pig but is distantly related to the elephant.

After Ch'enek, the traveller usually returns to Sankaber (three to four hours) and then Debark (five to six hours). But if arranged in advance, more extensive trips can be made to Buahit, at 4,437 metres (14,550 feet), which is outside the national park; Ras Dashen, Ethiopia's highest peak at 4,543 metres (14,901 feet); and the lowlands. Three game scout camps exist in the lowlands at Dirni, Muchila, and Adermas; but a trip here is a real expedition and recommended only for the more hardy people able to walk under tough conditions and cope with rock climbing. A trip from Ch'enek along the foot of the escarpment to the Wolkayit Pass and Debark lasts about five to seven days.

In Ethiopia's south-east lies the Bale Mountain range, which dominates the landscape as it rises from the extensive surrounding farmlands. At its epicentre is the spectacular Bale Mountains National Park, a high altitude plateau broken by numerous dramatic volcanic plugs and peaks, beautiful alpine lakes, and mountain streams that rush into deep, rocky gorges on their way to the lowlands below.

As one ascends into the mountains one will experience changes in the vegetation with altitude, from juniper forests to heather moorlands and alpine meadows — which at various times of the year exhibit an abundance of colourful wild flowers.

The national park is Africa's largest Afro-alpine habitat, with unlimited opportunities for some fantastic mountain walks, horse trekking, scenic driving, and the chance to view many of

Ethiopia's endemic mammals and birds.

Bale Mountains National Park is 2,400 square kilometres (1,488 square miles) in area, covering a wide range of habitats and ranging in altitude from 1,500 to 4,377 metres (4,920 to 14,357 feet), southern Ethiopia's highest point. The spectacular Harenna escarpment running from east to west divides the area into two major parts. To the north is a high-altitude plateau area, formed of ancient volcanic rocks and dissected by many rivers and streams that have cut deep gorges into the edges. In some places this has resulted in scenic waterfalls.

The vegetation here varies according to altitude. Around Dinsho, in the north, there are grass riverine plains, bordered by bands of bushes, particularly sagebrush and St. John's wort. Wild flowers, such as lobelia, geraniums, 'red-hot pokers', and *Alchemilla,* form carpets of colour. Higher up the mountains heather appears either as small bushes or as mature trees. The high Sanetti Plateau, at 4,000 metres (13,120 feet), is characterized by Afro-alpine plants, some coping with the extreme temperatures by becoming small and others by becoming large. The best example of the latter is the giant lobelia, whose stems stand high against the skyline.

Wild flowers are many and various, the dominant plant being the *Helichrysum,* or 'everlasting' flowers. The everlastings can be seen in many forms, but the grey bushes of *H. splendidum* are most striking, especially when covered with their yellow flowers. The vegetation on the plateau has to contend with the many species of rodents found here.

The southern part of the park is heavily forested after the

land falls away from the high plateau in a dense heather belt. The heather forest is particularly mature here, draped with many lichens.

The wildlife of Bale includes many endemic species. The park was originally established to protect two: the mountain nyala and the Simien fox (or jackal), which, despite its name, is more frequently seen in Bale than in the Simien Mountains National Park. The mountain nyala are best seen in the Gaysay area of the north where they spread out over the grass plains. Other wildlife in this area includes Menelik's bushbuck, an endemic sub-species in which the males are a very dark colour, numerous Bohor reedbuck, grey duiker, warthog, serval cat, colobus monkey, and Anubis baboon.

The high plateau is noted for the Simien fox, whose chestnut-red coat is in strong contrast to the grey vegetation. It preys on the numerous species of rodent found here, the biggest being the giant mole-rat. This subterranean animal, endemic to the Bale Mountains, can weigh as much as one kilo.

The forest of the south is so thick that animals are difficult to see, but there are three species of pig here — warthog, bushpig, and giant forest hog. There are also lion, leopard, spotted hyena, and, rarely, African hunting dog, which is normally found in a much more open habitat.

Bale's birds include sixteen endemic species, many of which are easily seen. These include wattled ibis, black-winged love-bird, blue-winged goose, Rouget's rail, and thick-billed raven. Wattled cranes are often seen breeding on the high plateau in the wet season.

There are three ways to explore the Bale Mountains National Park: by four-wheel drive vehicle, on foot, or on horseback — although the park is best suited for walking, being a mountainous and fragile environment.

If you choose to drive, there are nevertheless a few roads and tracks that can be negotiated with a four-wheel-drive vehicle.

A good area to explore first is Gaysay, which provides a good morning's or afternoon's wildlife watching and should not be missed by any visitor. Gaysay guarantees every visitor a chance to see the endemic mountain nyala in considerable numbers — as many as 400 have been seen here in a single afternoon. In addition, there are numerous grey duiker, warthog, and Menelik's bushbuck, with beautiful jet-black males. Colobus, serval cat, and baboon are sometimes seen as well. On very rare occasions leopard are sighted, and sometimes a pair of the endemic Simien fox. Birds abound, especially in the forest, and are usually heard if not seen.

Another spectacular drive is from Goba south to Dolo-Mena, across the eastern section of the national park and the Sanetti Plateau. This is the highest all-weather road in Africa and crosses the 4,000-metre (13,120-foot) contour through some of the loveliest mountain scenery on the continent that can be viewed from the comfort of a vehicle. It is even possible (but first check with rangers as to road conditions) to drive to the top of Tullu Deemtu — Ethiopia's second-highest mountain at 4,377 metres (14,357 feet).

The road climbs up from Goba through beautiful juniper and *Hagenia* forest and is lined with the orange-blossomed *Leonotis*.

Opposite: Trekkers and residents alike rely on the horse as the best means to get around the rugged terrain of the Bale Mountains.

Above: Limestone outcrop near Dinsho in the Bale Mountains.

Right: The 'Simien' fox, as it is widely known, is more often seen in the Bale Mountains than in the Simiens these days.

The forest gives way to giant St. John's wort woods — a narrow zone soon succeeded by heather moorlands. Then you are out of the forest and into the open, the mountains proper. Vistas reach out to the strange pinnacles of Chorchora Peak on the left — one of the park boundary markers — and across the sheer-sided Tegona River Gorge on the right.

Another steep zigzag climb across heather- and scrub-covered slopes leads to the plateau through portals of weird five-metre (16-foot) tall columns of giant lobelia. The plateau is studded with numerous shallow alpine lakes, with views to the steep-sided volcanic plug of Konteh Tullu to the south and the long, craggy ridges of Mount Batu — 4,203 metres (13,786 feet) — to the west.

The road continues climbing, gently now, past Crane lakes at the base on Konteh. This is the centre of the best area for seeing Simien fox and, on rare occasions, mountain nyala. The spectacular views can be even more awe-inspiring if you take the steep climb to the top of Konteh or the longer climb to the domed Tullu Deemtu summit to the west of the road soon after.

The main road continues south to the edge of the Harenna escarpment before descending through a series of breathtaking hairpin bends. The initial heather scrub gives way after a few kilometres to *Hagenia*, heather, and St. John's wort forest; later merging into lush *Podocarpus* forest: enormous trees covered with mosses, ferns, and 'old man's beard' lichens. This continues down the small Rira escarpment, where, looking back, one can see the tall Gujurule rock towers, their tops often shrouded in cloud and mist. Around their base is glorious mixed forest

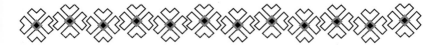

with bamboo and many clear, sparkling streams that are the source of the Shawe River, which the road later crosses before it suddenly ends, almost 100 kilometres (62 miles) from Goba.

The park boundary lies shortly before you cross the Shisha — a small tributary of the Yadot River. The forest gives way abruptly to dry, lowland wooded grasslands at about 1,600 metres (5,250 feet). About ten kilometres (six miles) later the little village of Dolo-Mena is reached. Here, on a market day, one will be treated to the surprising sight of camels — so soon after leaving the alpine conditions of more than 4,000 metres (13,120 feet).

Dolo-Mena is 110 kilometres (68 miles) from Goba, but a reasonable undertaking for a day's drive is from Goba to the plateau's southern edge, with perhaps a descent of the escarpment into the forest below, followed by a return to Goba. A good campsite exists at Katcha, after Rira on the left of the road, along a track to a quarry. This is a good base for walking in the bamboo forest and for exploring the Gujurule volcanic plugs.

A third track leads south from the park headquarters, crosses the interesting natural bridge over the Danka River, and runs beneath cliffs to the edge of the Web River Gorge. It ends in a broad, flat valley, from where it is an easy walk to the beautiful Finch'Abera waterfall.

Other 'supreme attractions' in Bale include the thirteen mountain streams and many ice-cold tarns that teem with fat and beautiful brown and rainbow trout. Stocked with fry from Kenya in the 1960s, these fish have flourished in the mountain waters and offer a challenge few fly-fishers could resist. Notable among the many options are the pools below the Upper Web falls and

Left: The endemic Menelik's bushbuck is much darker than other races of bushbuck and prefers high-altitude forest and bush.

Left: Another of Ethiopia's many endemic species, the stately mountain nyala, can only be found in the mountains of Bale and Arsi regions and in the Chercher Mountains in Harerge region.

Above: A typical bird of the moorlands of Ethiopia is the endemic Rouget's rail, common on the western and south-eastern highlands at higher elevations up to 4,100 metres.

Right: The Heberstreita dentata, *with its white, waxy blossoms, is one of many beautiful wild flowers to be found in the Bale Mountains.*

Addis Ababa

Caravan Travel & Tour Agency

the long, placid stretches where the river flows, green and crystal clear, across the moorlands. The self-help lodge at Dinsho is the Bale Trout Fishing Club headquarters.

Sof Omar: Caves of Wonder

Not far from Bale Mountains is one of the world's most spectacular and extensive underground caverns: the Sof Omar cave system. Formed by the Web River as it changed its course in the distant past and carved a new channel through limestone foothills, Sof Omar is an extraordinary natural phenomenon of breathtaking beauty.

Here, the Web River vanishes into this giant underground world, now an important Islamic shrine named after the saintly Sheikh Sof Omar, who took refuge here many centuries ago. It has a religious history that, in fact, predates the arrival of the Muslims in Bale — a history calibrated in thousands, not hundreds, of years.

The first religions in this part of Africa were essentially spirit worship and ghost cults in which the most powerful supernatural beings were believed to attach themselves to trees, rocks, and — most forcefully — to caves, which became shrines for prayer and sacrifice. Even today, the visitor to Sof Omar can see many signs of the persistence of such pagan beliefs and practices: a group of men sacrificing a goat; tokens of leather and cloth hung from rocky projections in the cave.

You approach the caves through the tiny village of Sof Omar, perched on the cliffs above the Web River. To the rear of the village is a dark, gaping crevice down which a precipitous narrow footpath winds to the first cave's floor. Only a few

Overleaf: Eerily enchanting, the Sof Omar cave system near the Bale Mountains has been an important Islamic shrine for centuries.

patches of sunlight filter into this dimly lit kingdom, which extends in all directions through vast subterranean passageways of polished white limestone, carved by the river's flood and recess over countless ages.

In this realm of dry, cool caves nature has worked a marvel of architecture — soaring pillars of stone twenty metres (66 feet) high, flying buttresses, fluted archways, and tall airy vaults. Finally, the river itself is reached, a sunless sea flowing through a deep gorge. Standing on a balcony near the roof, one has a spectacular view of the river rushing below.

Sof Omar's large central hall, the 'Chamber of Columns' — so named after the colossal limestone pillars that are its dominant feature — is one of the highlights of the cave system. At another part of the network there is a small gap in the rocks through which the river passes, about two and a half metres (eight feet) wide, where a bridge can be made with driftwood to go across. The most direct route through the caves passes these and many other remarkable sights, and takes about an hour at a good walking pace.

Inside the caves, the only living creatures are bats (which do not usually trouble the visitor) and fish. Crocodile are to be found in the river nearby but, fortunately, seem to shun the caves themselves. The countryside abounds with wildlife — dik-dik and kudu, serval cat, rock hyrax, giant tortoises, snakes, and lizards, as well as more than fifty species of birds.

Down the Rift Valley

One of Africa's most striking geographical features of Africa is a giant tear across the earth's surface visible even from space: the Great Rift Valley. Extending from the Middle East to Mozambique, the Rift Valley passes in a north-easterly to south-westerly direction right through Ethiopia, endowing the country with some spectacular sights that range from hot, dry, and barren places to a string of beautiful lakes.

This tremendous collapse of the earth's surface occurred at the same time that the Arabia Peninsula, geologically a part of Africa, was sundered from the rest of the continent.

Volcanic activity, which greatly contributed to the formation of the Rift Valley, continues up to present times. In Ethiopia, it finds expression in the presence of hot springs in many parts of the country, as well as volcanic cones in the Danakil Depression in the north-east.

The Danakil, or Afar, Depression, which encompasses a good portion of the eastern part of the Tigray region, is one of the earth's hottest and most inhospitable places, with many points more than 100 metres (328 feet) below sea level and noon-time temperatures soaring above 50°C (122°F). It is the site of a dry salt lake from which Ethiopians since time immemorial have obtained their *amoles*, or bars of salt, used both for consumption and, long ago, as a primitive sort of 'money'. Mined by the Afar people for at least a millenium and a half, the salt is loaded on camels and taken to the highlands, where it is still in considerable demand and fetches a good price.

The landscape of the Danakil seems carved from the infernos of hell and is a reminder of the furies that once ravaged this region,

with volcanic cones rising above the scabs of black lava. Earth tremors are frequent, and there are several still-active volcanoes in the area. Amazingly, there is also wildlife to be seen here, particularly zebra and wild ass.

And uninhabitable as this place may seem, it is nevertheless inhabited by thousands of Afar nomads. Tempestuous, proud, and individualistic, they live in small isolated groups and somehow manage to wrest a living — thanks to the salt — from this challenging and inhospitable wilderness. Using the camel as their beast of burden, they also keep sheep, goats, and cattle on the edge of the Danakil Desert or in the vicinity of the Awash River, where coarse grass grows.

The Awash River, in fact, is the central feature of two of Ethiopia's many wonderful national parks that follow the Rift Valley from the north-east to the south-west of the country.

Yangudi-Rassa National Park

The first, the Yangudi-Rassa National Park, is large — 4,730 square kilometres (2,933 square miles) — but little-developed. Temperatures are high and very little rain falls as the area is semi-desert — hence the vegetation is semi-arid grass and trees with succulent scrub. Yangudi-Rassa was created to protect the wild ass, an endangered species and ancestor of the domestic donkey. There are also gerenuk, Soemmerring's gazelle, Beisa oryx, Grevy's zebra and hamadryas baboon here — all indicators of the dry habitat.

Awash National Park

Also in this region is one of the country's most popular and interesting national parks: Awash, covering 827 square kilometres

Above: The Awash River cuts a path of green in an otherwise desolate landscape.

Right: Lone Grant's gazelle picks its way across the plains in the Awash National Park.

Opposite: The Danakil (Afar) region in north-eastern Ethiopia is an area of continuing seismic activity, with earth tremors frequently felt and several still active volcanoes.

(319 square miles). Its southern boundary is, in part, the Awash River.

One of the bonuses of the Awash National Park is that it is easily reached from the nation's capital, as it is situated in the lowlands only 211 kilometres (131 miles) to the east of Addis Ababa, on the main Addis-Assab highway, which bisects the park.

The main road from the town of Metehara leads to the park headquarters and the campsites, both of which are situated near the dramatic Awash Falls where the river enters its gigantic gorge.

The park is traversed by a series of well-maintained tracks, which take in the most spectacular of the many scenic attractions.

One of the main features is the Fantale volcano, on the southern flank of which can be seen the dark scar of the latest lava flow of 1820. The mountain slopes hold evidence of sixteenth-century habitation, seen as remains of walls and settlements of considerable proportion. The interior of the mountain-top crater — with its wispy white breath of steam vents — is still used by the local people, the Kereyu, for grazing livestock on a seasonal basis.

Another feature of the park are the hot springs in the extreme north. The water of these springs and rivers is in the region of 36°C (97°F) and is used by the local people to water stock. The unbelievably clear blue pools surrounded by doum palms invite the dusty traveller to wash off the day's dust — but be warned, they *are* hot.

The plains to the south of the main road are excellent for animal viewing and are bordered to the south by the Awash Gorge, plunging 250 metres (820 feet) to the river. The western end of the gorge is marked by the Awash Falls, which can vary in intensity from a murky reasonable flow to a raging chocolate-coloured torrent,

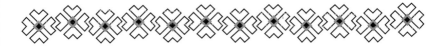

depending on the rainfall and the activity of the hydro-electric scheme above it.

Awash's wildlife reflects its dry nature. The Beisa oryx inhabits many of the more open areas, and greater and lesser kudu the bushed areas. Soemmerring's gazelle have distinctive white rumps and are often seen with the oryx. A small population of the endemic sub-species Swayne's hartebeest was translocated here and occupy the grass plains. The tiny Salt's dik-dik appears frequently under the dry acacia bushes and Defassa waterbuck are seen in the bushy river area. There are two species of baboon — the Anubis and the hamadryas. Though each has very different social structures, they hybridize near the river. Other monkeys are colobus in the riverine forest, and grivet in drier areas. Fantale crater provides a different habitat, supporting mountain reedbuck and klipspringer. Crocodile and hippopotamus splash in the Awash River and in the cooler parts of the springs and rivers in the north. Lion, leopard, serval, caracal, and wildcat are all seen infrequently.

The birds are numerous, more than 300 species on record. The campsites are an excellent place to sight birds. There, above the quiet murmur of the river, one can hear the exuberant chatter of green wood-hoopoes, the rollicking duet of red-and-yellow barbets, or the soft lament of the emerald-spotted wood dove — to name only a few. Carmine bee-eaters manoeuvre over the water, homing in on their airborne prey.

There are several bustard species in the park and secretary birds in the grass plains. The raptors are represented by fish eagles, tawny eagles, lanner and pygmy falcons, black-shouldered kites, and dark chanting goshawks. Bee-eaters and kingfishers provide splashes of

Below: Awash National Park's headquarters and campsite are situated near the dramatic Awash Falls, where the river enters its gigantic gorge.

Opposite: Family of Beisa oryx dash across a dusty road in Awash National Park.

Opposite bottom: Nature's artistic beauty captured in the spiralling horns of a young kudu.

colour, as do rollers. Ostriches roam the plains and the immense lammergeyer soars above Fantale searching for bones to smash.

Bordering the park, a twenty-eight-kilometre (17-mile) stretch of the Awash River offers a superb one- or two-day rafting trip — if the water level allows it — featuring lots of spirited rapids, wildlife, and impressive rugged cliffs and side canyons. The trip starts at the Awash Falls and ends at the beach below the town of Awash Station, with an optional overnight at a small hot springs sacred to the Kereyu people.

This north-eastern section of the Rift Valley is also home to two of Ethiopia's many fascinating markets: Senbete and Bati. Senbete is about halfway along the road from Addis Ababa to the Wollo region's capital of Dessie, while Bati is actually just past Dessie to the east. The drive to both witnesses some spectacular views of the Rift Valley, and the markets themselves are full of thousands of picturesque people selling and buying everything from camels and cows to clothing and coffee. It is a riot of colours and sounds; a not-to-be-forgotten experience.

But it is to the south-west of Addis Ababa that the remarkable topography of the Great Rift Valley really comes into view. Funnelled between two dramatic escarpments, this representation of the last great massive movement of the earth is home to a marvellous string of lakes: Ziway, Langano, Abijatta, Shalla, Awasa, Abaya, and Chamo — each with its own character; even those that lie side by side.

In addition to its chain of lakes, this south-western portion of the Ethiopian Rift also boasts a 'chain' of fascinating national parks: Abijatta-Shalla, Nechisar, Mago, and Omo.

Overleaf: Flamingos take flight over the waters of Lake Abijatta.

Five islands dot the surface of Lake Ziway, which — at 400 square metres (1,312 square feet) — is the largest in this 'northern cluster' of Rift Valley lakes. At least three of the islands were the site of medieval churches. The largest island — once known as Debre Tsion, or Mount of Zion, but now called Tullu Gudo — is still the site of a monastery, which holds a number of valuable illustrated manuscripts. In fact, the oldest written Ethiopian records about Axum were found here, supporting the belief that the islands were settled by Axumites who fled at the city's destruction.

The inhabitants, who for centuries practised terraced agriculture, speak a language of their own, close to that of the Gurage to the west and the Harari to the east. Many of the local people have reed boats similar to the *tankwas* that ply the waters of Lake Tana.

Because of the lake's many kinds of fish, a fishing station was set up in the area a few years ago. This has attracted a considerable number of water birds — including knob-billed geese, pelicans, and an occasional saddlebill stork — to the lake's edge, where they can easily be seen and photographed.

Lake Langano

The soft brown waters of Lake Langano — the next lake in the 'chain' — are set against the blue backdrop of the Arsi Mountains, which soar to 4,000 metres (13,120 feet). A few birds make Langano their home, but this resort is less for the nature lover than the water sports enthusiast and sun-worshipper. Although there are hippo, the crocodile population is fortunately small, and one can waterski, windsurf, sail, swim or bask in the blazing sun on the sloping sandy beaches.

Langano and nearby Lake Shalla are Ethiopia's only two lakes considered safe — bilharzia-free — for swimming. Despite its brown colour, Langano's water is clean and pleasant.

Abijatta-Shalla Lakes National Park

Using Lake Langano as a base, it is an easy side trip to visit the Abijatta-Shalla Lakes National Park, 887 square kilometres (550 square miles) in size — 482 (300) of it water.

Abijatta and Shalla are both terminal lakes but very different in nature. The surrounding area is mainly acacia woodland, some of which is very degraded by man. Lake Abijatta is a shallow pan, only fourteen metres (46 feet) deep, and its level fluctuates periodically, caused in part by human activity but often by natural phenomena as yet not fully understood. The beaches are unstable and saline, and vehicles must not venture too close as there is a very real danger of sinking.

Lake Shalla, by contrast, is, at 260 metres (853 feet), Ethiopia's deepest Rift Valley lake, possibly the deepest lake in Africa north of the Equator. It is an exceptionally beautiful and still largely untouched stretch of water, with several hot springs that bubble up by the shore and flow into the lake.

The sides are steep and rocky — often right down to the shore. Although swimming is considered safe, it may feel strange: the water's colour is like cold tea and there is a high concentration of salts, making it feel soapy. Few fish are found in this lake.

The park was created for the many aquatic bird species that use the lakes, particularly great white pelicans and greater and lesser flamingo. Shalla's islands are used as breeding sites by many birds,

and is home to the continent's most important breeding colony of great white pelicans. Because of the lake's lack of fish, the birds fly to Lake Abijatta — which has no islands — to feed. Other birds include white-necked cormorant, African fish eagle, Egyptian geese, various plover species, and herons. Although renowned for its bird life, Abijatta is now outclassed by Lake Awasa farther to the south.

Local mammals are not numerous but include Grant's gazelle — the northern limit for this species — greater kudu, oribi, warthog, and golden jackal.

To the south of Abijatta-Shalla lies the small 'paradise' of Wendo Genet, where an old but interesting hotel provides great views and an opportunity to bathe in the natural hot springs and small hot pool here, only a few metres from a cold, clear rushing mountain stream.

The Sidamo provincial capital of Awasa is situated on the shores of beautiful Lake Awasa. Enclosed by a gentle chain of mountains, the lake is an ideal spot for fishing and boating and is, as a result, one of the premier attractions in the Rift Valley lake chain.

A grassy dike built to contain the lake's steadily-rising water level is convenient for walks, sightseeing, and birdwatching — for which the lake is particularly known. The abundant storks and herons mingle with kingfishers, darters, plovers, wild ducks, Egyptian geese, crakes, and cormorants, creating a colourful spectacle. In a four-wheel-drive vehicle, it is possible — and pleasant — to drive all the way around the lake, where you will see a myriad of birds as well as picturesque Sidama villages.

Awasa town is an interesting attraction, with a bustling and attractive outdoor market that gives something of the flavour of the

50 YEARS

ETHIOPIAN AIRLINES

OF TRAIL-BLAZING

All we can give you

is the earth.

Fifty years after its first flight in April 1946 Ethiopian Airlines is still bringing Africa — and the world — together.

With the largest panAfrican route network of any airline, Ethiopian Airlines also flies daily to Europe, the Middle East and Asia.

Its intercontinental fleet of Boeing 767s and 757s and welcoming and friendly air crew make your flight the smoothest and most comfortable you'll ever experience.

And from the capital of Addis Ababa, aboard our new fleet, ETHIOPIAN takes you safely, smoothly and swiftly to wherever you wish to go in Ethiopia — a fascinating land with a recorded history of more than 3,000 years and home to the earliest of mankind's ancestors.

With almost 80 destinations within Ethiopia and worldwide the only sure way to discover Ethiopia is with Ethiopian Airlines.

Always out to serve!

region's life and commerce: horses, cattle, goats, and chickens are traded alongside lemons, tomatoes, green peppers, pungent spices, grains, sugar cane, and country butter wrapped in banana leaves.

Local markets are events not to be missed, if one happens to be travelling through a town on its particular weekly market day. In addition to Awasa, Wonago and Hagre Mariam have particularly picturesque and busy markets, with people from the many different ethnic groups in the region converging for business.

The most southerly of Ethiopia's lakes are Abaya and Chamo, which many consider to be the most beautiful lakes in the Rift Valley. Abaya, Ethiopia's longest and largest Rift Valley lake, lies just to the north of smaller but equally marvellous Lake Chamo. The two lakes are ringed by savannah plains and smoky mountain crests.

Nechisar National Park

Portions of the two lakes form an integral part of the Nechisar National Park, which is best explored from the provincial seat of Arba Minch.

From the town on the ridge of land that divides Abaya and Chamo there are commanding panoramic views all around, including both lakes with Nechisar on the eastern side and, to the west, the Guge range of mountains. The outstanding beauty of the neck of land between the two lakes has earned it the sobriquet of 'Bridge of Heaven'. The equally poetic Arba Minch — meaning 'forty springs' — takes its name from the bubbling streams which spring up amid the undergrowth of the luxuriant groundwater forest that covers the flats beneath the town. This alluring area is considered one of Ethiopia's last great surviving wilderness.

The shores and islands of Abaya and Chamo are populated by farming peoples such as the Ganjule and the Guji, both of whom also have ancient traditions of hippo hunting. The Guji ply the Lake Abaya waters in elegantly curved high-prowed *ambatch* boats similar to those depicted on the tombs of Egyptian pharaohs. Made of extremely light wood, an *ambatch* is capable of transporting several cattle at one time and is sufficiently sturdy to withstand any attack by crocodiles, which are present in large numbers — and large sizes — on both lakes.

The vivid contrasts of the Nechisar National Park will linger long in your memory — a swathe of white grass against the backdrop of clearly defined, deeply cut hills and mountains. From the escarpment on which Arba Minch stands you look down on the clear blue waters of Lake Chamo and the sandy beaches of its northern shores, covered by crocodiles lounging in the sun.

To the north, Lake Abaya's surface is a startling contrast of dark red, caused by the suspended load of ferrous hydroxide in its waters. At the base of the escarpment is a large area of groundwater forest around the Kulfo River, as well as the 'forty springs' after which Arba Minch is named. The western edge of the Rift Valley forms an impressive backdrop to the west.

Within the forest are shy, chestnut-red bushbuck, the comical bushpig, troops of Anubis baboons, and vervet monkeys.

The most commonly seen creatures of Nechisar's bush and savannah are two extremes of antelope: the large greater kudu,

Below: Lake Chamo is particularly known for its large and impressive crocodile population.

Opposite: The 'white grass' plains of the Nechisar National Park offer a strong contrast to the brown waters of Lake Abaya on one side and the blue waters of Lake Chamo on the other side.

Opposite bottom: Although the Nechisar plains at first seem surprisingly empty, they are dotted with herds of many species of game, including Burchell's zebra.

with its spectacular spiral horns and white-striped flanks, and the minuscule Guenther's dik-dik.

At first sight the Nechisar plains, which you encounter as you leave the peninsula between the two lakes, seem surprisingly empty. But dotting this apparently endless sweep of golden white grass are herds of Burchell's zebra, which mingle with Grant's gazelle and an occasional Swayne's hartebeest, an endemic subspecies. Also seen are black-backed jackal and African hunting dog.

The many and varied bird species reflect the different habitats within the park.

As well as their crocodiles and bird life, lakes Abaya and Chamo are famous for their sport fishing potential, especially for Nile perch — often weighing more than 100 kilos (220 pounds) — and for the fighting 'tiger fish'.

Winding up a trip down Ethiopia's section of the Rift Valley is not another lake, but a river.

Rising in the highlands south-west of Addis Ababa, the Omo River courses south for almost 1,000 kilometres (620 miles) but never reaches the sea. It is the sole feeder of Lake Turkana, East Africa's fourth largest lake, which the river enters just above the Kenyan border.

As it tumbles off the escarpment, the Omo passes from alpine environment and rain forest on into savannah country — and finally into searing desert lands. Through the millenia its flood-swollen waters have cut stupendous gorges. Wild game roam in abundance on both banks, while strange and colourful birds dart in and out of the lush vegetation.

Reckoned by enthusiasts to be one of Africa's premier locations for white water river rafting, its early fury takes it through gorges hundreds of metres deep and over formidable cataracts before it later snakes more peacefully amid dense jungles and finally across the colourful desert terrain. Its waters boil with fish and the huge shapes of crocodile and hippo.

Mago and Omo national parks
On the final leg of its journey south to Turkana, the Omo forms the border between Kefa and Gamo Gofa provinces. It's here that Ethiopia's largest nature sanctuary, the Omo National Park — one of the richest in spectacle and game and yet one of the least visited areas in East and Central Africa — is located. And another sanctuary, the Mago National Park, has been established on the eastern bank of the river: a land of endless, distant horizons.

Both parks can offer incredible spectacles of big game. Both have the merit, also, of being far from the beaten track and virtually unexplored, and thus are places in which game can be seen in a truly natural state.

Most easily accessed from the town of Jinka, Mago National Park is mainly savannah, with some forested areas around the rivers. It was set up to conserve the large numbers of plains animals in the area, particularly buffalo, giraffe, and elephant. Also seen here are topi and lelwel hartebeest, as well as lion, leopard, Burchell's zebra, gerenuk, and greater and lesser kudu. The birds are also typical of the dry grassland habitat, featuring bustards, hornbills, weavers, and starlings. Kingfishers and herons feed in and around the Neri River, which provides an

Below: Exciting moments as rafters negotiate one of the Omo River's biggest rapids, Potamus Plunge.

Left, top to bottom: Lake Shalla is home to Africa's most important breeding colony of great white pelicans; The extensive wilderness areas of Mago and Omo national parks harbour a wide range of big game, including the impressive African lion; Large herds of the African buffalo can be found in both Mago and Omo national parks.

Above: Beautiful birds — such as this malachite kingfisher — abound near Ethiopia's Rift Valley lakes.

alternative habitat.

Although adjoining Mago, the large and beautiful Omo National Park has been hardly visited in the last two decades, as getting there has been so difficult.

The only access to the park is via Omo Rate, by ferry to the west bank of the Omo River, and north to the border settlement of Kibish, where an unmaintained seventy-five-kilometre (46-mile) track leads to the Omo Park headquarters. However, the long-neglected route from Mui River up to Maji, tenuously linked to the town of Jimma, is being worked on. When this road is passable, a drive from Jimma — besides being extremely interesting in itself — will bestow the reward of visiting this truly wild and untamed area.

The parks are extensive wilderness areas and wildlife can be prolific: large herds of eland and buffalo, elephant, giraffe, cheetah, lion, leopard, and Burchell's zebra. Lesser kudu, lelwel hartebeest, topi, and oryx are all resident species, as well as deBrazza's and colobus monkeys and Anubis baboon. The 306 bird species recorded include many that will be familiar to East African visitors.

Southern peoples and cultures

Wildlife and beautiful scenery aside, this part of the country is home to many diverse and fascinating peoples and cultures: the Dorze, famed for their intricately woven houses and their woven cotton cloth; the Konso, who for centuries have practised terracing and intensive agriculture in their steep land and are known for the eerie wooden totems they erect over the graves of the dead.

The lower Omo is home to an astonishing mix of small, contrasting ethnic groups — the Bume, the Karo, the Galeb, the Bodi, the Mursi, the Surma, the Arbore, and the Hamar, to name only a few.

Lacking any material culture and artifacts common to more 'civilized' peoples, these tribes find unique ways in which to express their artistic impulses.

The Surma and the Karo, for example, are experts at body painting — using clays and locally available vegetable pigments to trace fantastic patterns on one another's faces, chests, arms, and legs.

These designs do not appear to have any special significance but are created purely for fun and aesthetic effect — each artist vying to outdo his fellows.

Scarification, on the other hand — also popular among most peoples of the lower Omo — does contain a number of specific symbolic messages. Mursi warriors carve deep crescent incisions on their arms to represent each enemy they have killed in battle.

Elaborate hairstyles are another form of personal adornment. Hamar women wear their hair in dense ringlets smeared with mud and clarified butter and topped off with a head-dress featuring oblongs of gleaming aluminium; Galeb and Karo men sculpt and shave their hair into extravagant shapes, with special ochre 'caps' of hair usually containing several ostrich feathers.

Jewellery tends to be simple but striking — colourful necklaces, chunky metal wristlets and armlets, shiny nails appended to skirts, multiple earrings, and so on.

The insertion of wooden and terra-cotta disks into the ear

Above left: The Mursi are well known for the large clay discs that the women wear, inserted in their slit lower lips. These lip plates — and similar ear lobe discs — constitute important distinctions of female beauty in Mursi society.

Above: Nuer women, as well as men, favour decorative skin scarification, with a spike of ivory or brass thrust through the lower lip.

Left: Hamer women wear their hair in dense ringlets smeared with mud and clarified butter and topped off with a head-dress featuring oblongs of gleaming aluminium. String upon string of cowrie shell necklaces are worn for further adornment.

lobes is a widespread custom. Mursi and Surma women also progressively split and stretch their lower lips to make room for similar disks there, too. Though these 'lip plates' may appear bizarre to outsiders, the Mursi and Surma themselves regard them as signs of beauty — generally speaking, the larger the lip plate the more desirable the wearer.

Gambella National Park

Although not technically in the Rift Valley, the only of Ethiopia's national parks not yet mentioned — Gambella National Park — lies along another of the country's important rivers: the Baro. Near the town of Gambella, Gambella National Park, is one of Ethiopia's least developed parks and has no facilities. Nevertheless, the large conservation area contains many species not found elsewhere in the country, such as the Nile lechwe and the white-eared kob. Roan antelope, topi, elephant, buffalo, giraffe, and the unusual whale-headed stork are also to be found here.

The people of this area are the Anuak and the Nuer. Mainly fisherfolk — but also cattle herders — the Anuak and Nuer are extremely handsome, with dark, satiny complexions. Both men and women favour a style of decorative scarification on the chest, stomach, and face; and often boast heavy bone bangles, bright bead necklaces, and spikes of ivory or brass thrust through a hole pierced in the lower lip and protruding down over the chin.

Unaffected by the ways of the modern world — so near, yet so far from them — these interesting people remain as remote, unchanged, and beautiful as the land in which they live.

When travelling in Ethiopia as a tourist or businessman there are two things that you will soon realize are complete:

COMMERCIAL BANK OF ETHIOPIA

P O Box 255, Addis Ababa, Ethiopia
Tel: 251-515004; 251-1-515028
Fax: 251-1-514522; 251-1-517822

1 That Charles Darwin's theory of human ancestors' missing link is complete with archeological discoveries of

   a) Ramidas, 4.4 million years old (latest find)

   b) Lucy, 3.5 million years old (with more compact bones and skeletal build)

2 That your money-check-transactions at the Commercial Bank of Ethiopia are complete with

   a) More than half a century old expediency, quite a rich experience in banking activity

   b) 155 branches scattered throughout the length and breadth of the country

Ethiopia In Brief

Ethiopia:
One of the few African countries never to lose its independence, Ethiopia is as large as France and Spain combined and has one of the richest histories on the African continent.

Addis Ababa:
The capital was settled in 1886 and christened by Queen Taytu, consort of Menelik II. The population according to the last official census was 1.4 million; recent estimates have it at closer to five million.

Towns:
The second-largest town in Ethiopia is Dire Dawa, with a population of 99,980 in 1984. Gondar is the third-largest town, with a population of 80,675 in 1984.

People:
The 1984 census recorded a national population of 42.6 million, although that included the now separate nation of Eritrea. Although no official census has been taken since then, the population of Ethiopia today is estimated to be approximately 55 million. Approximately 26 per cent are under the age of 14 and almost half are under 34.

Religion:
The major religions are Christianity (Ethiopian Orthodox Church) and Islam.

Language:
Amharic is the official language of Ethiopia, although English, Italian, French, and Arabic are widely spoken. In areas outside of the larger cities and towns, indigenous languages are likely to be spoken — of which there are eighty-three, with some 200 dialects. The most common of these are Orominya and Tigrinya.

Climate:
Despite its proximity to the Equator, Ethiopia's high altitude ensures a temperate, moderate, even chilly climate — certainly not tropical. There are two rainy seasons: the irregular short rains from late January to early March, and the long rains from June until mid-September.

Government:
Ethiopia is an independent republic operating under the Transitional Government of Ethiopia. The president is the head of state, while the prime minister is the head of government.

Entry points by air:
Bole International Airport, Addis Ababa; minor airfields include those at Dire Dawa, Bahar Dar, and Gondar.

Entry points by rail:
Dewele on the Djibouti border. Arrivals undergo full customs and immigration checks. The railway, with day and night trains, runs from Addis Ababa to Djibouti via Nazaret, Awash Station, and Dire Dawa.

Entry points by road:
Moyale (in Kenya), Humera and Metema (in Sudan), and Dewele (in Djibouti). All have full customs and immigration checks.

Calendar:
Ethiopia follows the Julian calendar, which consists of twelve months of thirty days each and a thirteenth month of five days (six days in a leap year). The calendar is seven years and eight months behind the Western (Gregorian) calendar.

Communications:
Telephone, telex, fax, and airmail services connect Addis Ababa to all parts of the world. Services are available at the General Post Office and its many branches, as well as in the main hotels. International direct dialling is available from all major centres in the country.

Currency:
The local currency is the Ethiopian birr, made up of 100 cents. Notes are issued in denominations of 1, 5, 10, 50, and 100 birr. There are five different coins: 1, 5, 10, 25, and 50 cents.

Currency regulations:
There is no limit to the amount of foreign currency imported into Ethiopia, but it must be declared on arrival, using a currency declaration form. Foreign currency may be changed only at authorized banks and hotels. The currency declaration form will be required by Customs on departure. Visitors may change back any excess birr into foreign currency at the airport before departure, but you must, in addition to the currency declaration form, bring with you all receipts for exchange transactions.

Daylight:
Being relatively close to the Equator, there is an almost constant twelve hours of daylight. In Addis Ababa, the sunrise and sunset start at around 06.30 and 18.45 respectively.

Departure tax:

The airport departure tax is US$ 10, payable in any
convertible currency. Traveller's cheques are not
acceptable. On local flights, there is a 'boarding charge'
of five birr for residents and non-residents alike.

Driving:

Drivers require a valid International Driving Licence,
which can be obtained by exchanging your local licence
at the Transport and Communications office on Asmara
Road in Addis Ababa. Visitors can recover their original
licences a day or so prior to departure. Those with their
own vehicles will require a permit from the Ministry of
Transport and Communications. Driving is on the right.

Energy:

Ethiopia uses 220 volts and 50 Hz. It is best to bring your
own round, two-prong adapter and transformer if
necessary.

Health requirements:

All visitors (including infants) are required to possess a
valid yellow fever vaccination certificate. Vaccination
against cholera is also required for any person who has
visited or been in transit through a cholera-infected
area within six days prior to arrival in Ethiopia. Malaria is
endemic throughout the country. Visitors should begin
taking a recommended chloroquine-based prophylactic
two weeks before their arrival and continue taking them
for six weeks after their departure. In addition,
medication for chloroquine-resistant malaria is a wise
precaution.

Medical services:

Medical facilities are limited and of generally poor
standard. Existing facilities are sorely overtaxed.
Tourists and non-citizen residents should go to private
hospitals and clinics. Contact your embassy for referral
to a recommended doctor. Air rescue services are
available, and you might want to make arrangements
with one before your trip.

Time:

Ethiopia is three hours ahead of Greenwich Mean
Time. Time remains constant throughout the year.
The Ethiopian day is calculated in a manner similar to
many equatorial countries, where day and night are
always the same length: counting starts at Western 6.00
a.m. and 6.00 p.m. Western 7.00 a.m. is therefore one
o'clock, noon is six, 6.00 p.m. is twelve o'clock
midnight, and so on.

Visa and immigration requirements:

Visa applications may be obtained at Ethiopia's
diplomatic missions in Abidjan, Accra, Beijing,
Bonn, Brussels, Cairo, Dakar, Djibouti, Geneva,
Harare, Jeddah, Khartoum, Lagos, London, Moscow,
Nairobi, New Delhi, New York City, Ottawa, Paris,
Pyongyang, Riyadh, Rome, Sanaa, Seoul, Stockholm,
Tel Aviv, Tehran, Tokyo, Tripoli, Vienna, and
Washington DC. Visas are required for all visitors to
Ethiopia, with the exception of nationals of Djibouti,
Eritrea, Kenya, and Sudan.

Endemic mammals:

Gelada baboon, Starck's hare, Giant molerat, Simien
fox, Menelik's bushbuck, mountain nyala, Swayne's
hartebeest, Walia ibex.

Endemic birds:

Wattled ibis, blue-winged goose, Harwood's
francolin, Rouget's rail, spot-breasted plover, white-
collared pigeon, black-winged lovebird, yellow-
fronted parrot, Prince Ruspoli's turaco, golden
backed woodpecker, Degodi lark, Sidamo long-
clawed lark, white-tailed swallow, Abyssinian
longclaw, white-winged cliffchat, Ruppell's chat,
Abyssinian catbird, white-backed black tit, yellow-
throated seed-eater, Ankober seed-eater, Salvadori's
seed-eater, black-headed siskin, white-billed starling,
black-headed forest oriole, Stresemann's bush crow,
thick-billed raven.

National parks:

Abijatta-Shalla Lakes National Park, Shewa region
Awash National Park, Shewa/Arsi regions
Bale Mountains National Park, Bale region
Gambella National Park, Ilubabor region
Mago National Park, Gamo Gofa region
Nechisar National Park, Gamo Gofa region
Omo National Park, Kaffa region
Simien Mountains National Park, Gondar region
Yangudi-Rassa National Park, Hararge region

Wildlife sanctuaries:

Babille Elephant Sanctuary, Hararge region
Kuni-Muktar Mountain Nyala Sanctuary, Hararge region
Senkele Swayne's Hartebeest Sanctuary, Shewa region
Yabello Sanctuary, Sidamo region

Principal museums and historical sites:

Addis Ababa Museum, Addis Ababa
Addis Alem Maryam Museum, Addis Alem
Awash National Park Museum, Awash
Axum Museum, Axum
Church of Saint Mary of Zion, Axum
Church of Saint Mary, Addis Alem
Debre Damo Monastery, Debre Damo
Enda Kirkos, Wukro
Entoto Museum, Entoto Mountain, near Addis Ababa
Ethnological Museum, Addis Ababa
Hadar Archaeological Site, Awash Valley
Harar, Harerge region (ancient walled city)
Harar Community Museum, Harar
Harar Government Museum, Harar
Lake Tana monasteries, Gondar/Gojjam regions
Lego Dooa, Dire Dawa (rock paintings)
Makale Museum, Makale
Melka Konture Archaeological Site, Awash River
Nagash, Tigray (ancient Islamic town)
National Archaeological Museum, Addis Ababa
National Postal Museum, Addis Ababa
Natural History Museum, Addis Ababa
Park of the Stelae, Axum
Porc Epic Cave, Dire Dawa (rock paintings)
Rock-hewn Churches of Lalibela
Saint George's Church Museum, Addis Ababa
Sanctuary Chapel, Axum (said to house Ark of the
Covenant)
Sof Omar Caves, Bale
Temple of the Moon, Yeha
Tiya Silte Megalithic Site, Sidamo

Other historical sites:

Abba Daniel (Korkor), near Dugum, Tigray (rock
church)
Abiy Addi Mikael, near Dugum, Tigray (rock church)
Abraha and Atsbaha, near Wukro, Tigray (rock church)
Abu Said Tomb, Harar (historical)
Abuna Tekle Haymanot, Hauzien, Tigray (rock church)
Adadi Mariam Church, near Addis Ababa (rock church)
Amba Mikael, near Haiki Meshal, Tigray (rock church)
Ankober Palace ruins, Ankober
Arba Minch Museum, Arba Minch
Arbatu Entzessa, Wollo (rock church)
Arbatu Insisa, near Senkata, Tigray (rock church)
Barka, near Atsbi, Tigray (rock church)
Bilbila Giyorgis, Wollo (rock church)
Birgida Maryam Church, Lake Tana
Church of Debre Tabor, Debre Tabor
Church of Heruy Giyorgis, Debre Tabor
Debre Genet Monastery, Makale
Debre Maar Giyorgis, near Dugum, Tigray (rock church)
Debre Maryam (Korkor), near Dugum, Tigray (rock
church)
Debre Selam, near Atsbi, Tigray (rock church)
Debre Sion, near Dugum, Tigray (rock church)
Dega Estafanos Musem, Dega Estafanos Monastery, Lake
Tana
Djima Museum, Djima
Dugum Maryam Airefeda, near Dugum, Tigray (rock
church)
Dugum Selassie, near Dugum, Tigray (rock church)
Enda Gabriel, near Senkata, Tigray (rock church)
Enda Medhane Alem, near Senkata, Tigray (rock
church)
Enda Midael (Biet Maar), near Senkata, Tigray (rock
church)
Enda Mikael (Melhai Zenghi), near Senkata, Tigray
(rock church)
Enda Yesus Fort, Makale
Gebre-Meskel Tomb, near Axum
Grand Mosque, Harar
Guh Korkor (Abba Yemata), near Dugum, Tigray (rock
church)
Gulubsha Maryam, near Dugum, Tigray (rock church)
Gundefru, near Haiki Meshal, Tigray (rock church)
Kebran Gabriel Monastery, Lake Tana
King Bazen Tomb, near Axum
Liche ruins, near Debre Birhan
Lioness of Gobedra rock carving, near Axum
Maitsebri Arbatu Insisa, near Dugum, Tigray (rock
church)
Maryam Church, Ankober
Maryam Church, Entoto
Maryam Barakeet, near Dugum, Tigray (rock church)
Maryam Papaseiti, near Dugum, Tigray (rock church)
Medhane Alen Church, Ankober
Menelik's residence, Addis Alem
Mikael Aragawi, near Dugum, Tigray (rock church)
Mikael Menda, near Dugum, Tigray (rock church)
Welega Museum, Nekemte
Na'akuto La'ab, Wollo (rock church)
Petros and Paulos, near Senkata, Tigray (rock church)
Queen of Sheba's Grave, near Axum
Queen of Sheba's Palace ruins, near Axum
Raguel Church, Entoto
Ramha Tomb, Axum
Ras Makonnen Palace, Harar
Rimbaud House, Harar
Saint Michael's Church, near Addis Ababa (rock
church)
Sarsana Mika'el, Wollo (rock church)
Tullu Gudo Monastery, Lake Ziway
Ura Kidane Mehret Monastery, Lake Tana
Wollo Museum, Dessie
Yaed Kidane Mehret, near Dugum, Tigray (rock church)
Yemrehanna Krestos, Wollo (rock church)
Yohannes Meakuddi, near Dugum, Tigray (rock church)

Ethiopia missions abroad:

Austria: Friedrich Schmidtplatz 3/3, A-1080, Vienna; Tel: 4028410-12; Fax: 4028413

Belgium: PO Box Clos Henrivaes, 5, Brussels; Tel: 7348762/7339817; Fax: 7321851

Canada: 112 Kent Street, Suite 208, Tower B, Ottawa, Tel: 2356637; Fax: 2354638

Djibouti: Rue Clochette, PO Box 230, Djibouti; Tel: 350718/353711; Fax: 354803

Egypt: 32 Ibrahim Osman Street, PO Box 12, Midan Bahlawi Dokki, Cairo; Tel: 3477805/3466909; Fax: 3479002

France: 35, Avenue Charles Floquet, 75007, Paris; Tel: 47838395, Fax: 43065214

Germany: Brentano Strasse 1, PO Box 5300 Bonn 1, Bonn; Tel: 233041–43; Fax: 233015

Israel: 69 Bugrashov Street, 63429, Tel Aviv; Tel: 5250406; Fax: 5250428

Italy: Via Andrea Vesalio, PO Box 16-1800161, Rome; Tel: 4403652/4403635; Fax: 4403676

Japan: 2-16-12, Jamigaya, Shibuya-ku, Tokyo 151; Tel: 3718-1003, 1005, 1018; Fax: 3718-0978

Kenya: PO Box 45198, Nairobi; Tel: 723035/723027; Fax: 723401

Korea, South, Republic of: Hannam Dong Yong, Son Ku Seoul; Tel: 7908927/8; Fax: 7908929

Nigeria: PO Box 2488, Mariana, Lagos; Tel: 2615055; Fax: 2613198

Russia: Orlovo Davydusky - Per 6, PO Box 129041, Moscow; Tel: 2801010/2801676; Fax: 2806608

Senegal: PO Box 379, Dakar; Tel: 243728; Fax 243727

Saudi Arabia: Maiaz, University Street, PO Box 94341, Riyadh; Tel: 4775285; Fax: 4768020, OR PO Box 495, Jeddah; Tel: 6653411/6605034, Fax: 6653413

South Africa: Lynn Wood, Farmer's Folly 26, Pretoria; Tel: 3489242; Fax: 476773

Sweden: Ostemalams Gatan 34, PO Box 26116, Stockholm; Tel: 6656030/6609166; Fax: 6608177

Switzerland: 56 Rue de Millebeau, 1211 Geneva 19; Tel: 7330758/7330759/3628001; Fax: 7401129

United Kingdom: 17 Prince's Gate, SW1 1PZ, London; Tel: 5897212/5846984; Fax: 5847054

United States of America: 866 United Nations Plaza, New York; Tel: 4211830-34; Fax: 7540360, OR 2154 Kalorama Road NW, Washington DC, 20008; Tel: 2342281/2342282-4; Fax: 3287950

Yemen: Hadda Road, PO Box 234, Sanaa; Tel: 208833; Fax: 213780

Zimbabwe: 14, Lenark, Belegravia, PO Box 2745, Harare; Tel: 725822/23; Fax: 720259

Ethiopian Airlines Offices Abroad:

Canada: Tel: 416-922-1526, Toronto.

Djibouti, Republic of: Rue de Marseille, Box 90, Djibouti; Tel: 351007/354235.

Egypt: Nile Hilton, Box 807, Cairo; Tel: 5740603/5740911.

France: 25, Rue de Ponthieu, 75008, Paris; Tel:

53760538; Fax: 53760537.

Germany: Am Hauptbahnhof 6, 60329 Frankfurt Am Main; Tel: 2740070; Fax: 27400730.

Greece: 17, Fillelinon Street, Athens, 10557; Tel: 322-4447/322-4551/322-4553; Fax: 322-4586.

Italy: Via Paolo da Cannobio 33, Milan; Tel: 8056562/86450270; Fax: 72010638 OR Via Barberini 51, Rome; Tel: 4819377.

Japan: Daido Seimei Building, 2F, 2-7-4 Nihonbashi Chuo-Ku, Tokyo 103; Tel: 1990; Fax: 1889.

Kenya: Muindi Mbingu Street, Box 42901, Nairobi; Tel: 330837/330846; Fax: 219007,

Netherlands, The: Stadhouderskade 2, 6th Floor, 1054 ES Amsterdam; Tel: 6839819/6839723; Fax: 6850501

Oman, Sultanate of: Box 962, Muscat; Tel: 796976/796987; Fax: 796987.

Saudi Arabia: Medina Road, Box 8913, Jeddah, 21492; Tel: 6512365/6512996; Fax: 6516670 OR Al Zouman Center, Old Airport Road, PO Box 7543, Riyadh, 11472; Tel: 4782140/4789763; Fax: 4793155.

South Africa: 1st Floor East Wing, Jorrisen Place, St. Braamfontein-2017, Box 30693, Johannesburg; Tel: 403-2762-3; Fax: 339-6348.

Sweden: Kungsgatan 44, 11135, Stockholm; Tel: 4111826/4111829; Fax: 205524.

Switzerland: 9, Rue du Mont-Blanc, Geneva; Tel: 732-1926; Fax: 731-5089.

Thailand: 10/12-13 S.S. Building, 2nd Floor, Convent Road, Bangkok, 10500; Tel: 933-4714/233 6744/233-8950-4; Fax: 236-7186.

United Arab Emirates: Sheikh Hamdan Ave, Box 346, Abu Dhabi; Tel: 333323/333342; Fax: 317012 OR Flat 202, Pearl Building, Benyas Street, Box 7140, Dubai, Tel: 237963/237987/284338; Fax: 273306/241841.

United Kingdom: 4th Floor, Foxglove House, 166 Piccadilly, London W1V 9DE; Tel: 071-491-9119; Fax: 071-491-1892.

United States: California: Tel: 213-462-7901, Los Angeles OR Tel: 415-668-4275, San Francisco. Colorado: Tel: 303-534-0999, Denver. Florida: Tel: 800-445-2733, Miami. Georgia: Tel: 800-445-2733, Atlanta. Massachusetts: Tel: 800-445-2733, Boston. Illinois: 320 N. Michigan Avenue, Chicago, 60601; Tel: 312-368-0555 or 800-433-9677; Fax: 312-368-8490. New York: 405 Lexington Avenue, New York, 10174; Tel: 212-867-0095 or 800-445-2733; Fax: 212-692-9589. Texas: Tel: 214-263-1993, Dallas OR Tel: 713-654-9055, Houston. Washington (state): Tel: 206-467-1885, Seattle. Washington DC: Tel: 800-445-2733.

Yemen: Ali Abdul Moghni Street, Box 161, Sanaa, Tel: 272437; Telex: 2243.

Zimbabwe: Cabs Center, 4th Floor, Cnr Jason Moyo Avenue, 2nd Street, Box 1332, Harare; Tel: 790705-6/795215-6; Fax: 795216.

ADDIS ABABA

H I L T O N

"Take me to the Hilton."

The Addis Ababa Hilton is set in 15 acres of landscaped gardens

ADDIS ABABA HILTON: Tel: (251-1) 518400 • PO Box 1164 Addis Ababa, Ethiopia
CABLE HILTELS, ADDIS ABABA • Telex: 21104 • Fax No: (251-1) 510064

Major Hotels in Addis Ababa:

Airport Motel, PO Box 100520; Tel: 188222; Fax: 610577
Axum Hotel, PO Box 40318; Tel: 613916; Fax: 614265
Bekele Mola Hotels, PO Box 1349; Tel: 514601; Fax: 518223
Central Shewa Hotel, PO Box 21352; Tel: 611454; Fax: 610063
Central Venue Hotel, PO Box 5695; Tel: 163289; Fax: 710744
City Hotel, PO Box 33185; Tel: 755249
Crown Hotel, PO Box 101299; Tel: 341046; Fax: 341428
Ethiopia Hotel, PO Box 1131; Tel: 517400; Fax: 510871
Extreme Hotel, PO Box 6948; Tel: 553777; Fax: 551077
Ghion Hotel, PO Box 1643; Tel: 513222; Fax: 510278
Goye Hotel, PO Box 6223; Tel: 710987
Hilton International, PO Box 1164; Tel: 518400; Fax: 510064
Holiday Hotel, PO Box 258; Tel: 612081; Fax: 612627
Ibex Hotel, PO Box 21429; Tel: 654400; Fax: 653737
Imperial Hotel, PO Box 2966; Tel: 181190; Fax: 614493
Motera Hotel, PO Box 9470; Tel: 754633; Fax: 755299
Plaza Hotel, PO Box 4935; Tel: 612200; Fax: 613044
Ras Hotel, PO Box 1632; Tel: 517060; Fax: 517327
Sheraton Addis, PO Box 6002; Tel: 517138; Fax: 514029
Wabe Shebelle Hotel, PO Box 3154; Tel: 517187; Fax: 518477
Yordanos Hotel, PO Box 1647; Tel: 512470; Fax: 516655

Major Tour Operators in Ethiopia:

Abyssinia Tours, PO Box 100355, Addis Ababa; Tel: 614240; Fax: 614240
AKI Tour Co., PO Box 5923, Addis Ababa; Tel: 654889; Fax: 511699
Al-TAD Ethiopia P.L.CO., PO Box 1223, Addis Ababa; Tel: 513755; Telex: 21981; Fax: 515244
Ambassador Abdulmenan Sheka; PO Box 41103, Addis Ababa; Tel: 158186; Fax: 514139
Ato Amsal Getenet (Dashen International Travel Agency and Tour Operator), PO Box 101568, Addis Ababa; Tel: 513305; Fax: 605452
Caravan Tours, PO Box 1348, Addis Ababa; Tel: 516501; Telex: 21506; Fax: 517454
Dimitris Assimalopalos Safari, PO Box 2437, Addis Ababa; Tel: 516616; Telex: 21946; Fax: 517334
Eastern Travel & Tourist Agency, PO Box 1136, Addis Ababa; Tel: 511574; Fax: 511468
Ethio Rift Valley Safari, PO Box 3658, Addis Ababa; Tel: 551127; Telex: 21245; Fax: 550298
Experience Ethiopia Travel (EET), PO Box 9354, Addis Ababa; Tel: 152336/519291; Fax: 519982
Explore Ethiopia Travels P.L.C., PO Box 6770, Addis Ababa; Tel: 653961; Fax: 653862
Galaxy Travel Services, PO Box 1128, Addis Ababa; Tel: 510355; Telex: 21949; Fax: 511236

Ghion Nile Touring Investment, PO Box 3228, Addis Ababa; Tel: 512524; Fax: 519777/513553
Hess Travel Ethiopia P.L.C., PO Box 1569, Addis Ababa; Tel: 111252
Life Lion General Trading and Travel Tourism P.L.C., PO Box 59002, Addis Ababa; Tel: 518872
Lift Air Ethiopia, PO Box 5609, Addis Ababa; Tel: 518715; Fax: 519601
Maj. Gizaw Gedle Giorges Safari, PO Box 5218, Addis Ababa; Tel: 200824; Telex: 21386
Mitchel Cotts Co., PO Box 527, Addis Ababa; Tel: 517160; Telex: 21036; Fax: 515365
National Tour Operation & Travel Agency, PO Box 5709, Addis Ababa; Tel: 512955; Telex: 21370; Fax: 517688
Nile Touring Co., PO Box 4090, Addis Ababa; Tel: 513553; Telex: 21247; Fax: 753611
Number Nine Travel Agency, PO Box 4737, Addis Ababa; Tel: 551787; Telex: 21423; Fax: 551787
ORORO, PO Box 31627, Addis Ababa; Tel: 112207; Telex: 21104; Fax: 551277
Rockey Valley Colonel Nigussie Eshete Tour & Photo Safari, PO Box 22867, Addis Ababa; Tel: 127436; Fax: 517454
Travel Ethiopia P.L.C., PO Box 9438, Addis Ababa; Tel: 150040/150036; Fax: 510200/551276
Wild Life Safaris Ethiopia, PO Box 2444; Addis Ababa; Tel: 553767; Fax: 551276
Yumo International Agency, PO Box 5698, Addis Ababa; Tel: 518878; Telex: 21313; Fax: 513451

NTO, the oldest and most reliable Tour Operator and Travel Agent in Ethiopia, offers Group and Individual Tours, including:-

- Special interest tours
- Historical tours
- Photo safaris
- Bird-watching and Nature tours
- Half day or full day tours of Addis Ababa NTO's fleet of 137 vehicles has the latest Mercedes luxury tourist buses, station wagons, 4-wheel-drives, medium and mini buses, pickups, etc.

We provide:-

- Transfer services
- Ticketing and air booking
- Taxi service with luxury Mercedes automobiles stationed outside major hotels and at the airport
- Car hire
- Professional guide services
- SAFARI outfitting that makes you feel in town in the bush!!

Our branch offices at Axum, Bahar Dar, Dire Dawa, Gondar, Lalibela and Mekele host our customers. **NTO** is the representative of American Travel related services. **NTO** honours American Express cards.

NTO's resources, the dedication and special care of our staff to our customers make us the leading and most reliable **TOUR OPERATOR** in Ethiopia. Tell us what you would like . . . and we will do our best. If you expect the best then make us your choice. With our service you can see Ethiopia at its best.

የብሔራዊ አስጎብኚና የጉዞ ወኪል ድርጅት

Throughout The Land of 13 Months of Sunhine

National Tour Operation and Travel Agency Enterprise PO Box 5709, Addis Ababa
Tel: (251-1) 514838/512923/ 159274/ 512955/ 152628/ 156109 Fax: (251-1) 51 76 88 Tlx: 21370 NTO ZZ ET
Branches: Axum. Bahar Dar, Dire Dawa, Gondar, Lalibela, Mekele.

Sheraton Addis

THE LUXURY COLLECTION

AT LAST A CHOICE

The Sheraton Addis
Welcomes you to Ethiopia

Discover a world of difference at the new
Sheraton Hotel in Addis Ababa.
The unsurpassed quality in the 295 room hotel
will turn any business trip into a breathtaking visit to
remember.
The property offers a wide selection of exquisite
accommodation; an executive floor, 33 suites including
a presidential suite and ten luxury villas, each with its
own private swimming pool.
The main hotel offers an endless array of dining options
including Italian, Indian and Gourmet cuisine. There is a
wide variety of recreational activities available
including a magnificient pool area, four squash courts,
four tennis courts and private health club. Blend the
warmth and hospitality of the Ethiopian people with a
reputation for excellence in service, food,
accommodation and amenities. Bring all this together
under one name.

THE LUXURY COLLECTION
ITT SHERATON

General Contractor: Al-Tad Construction PLC
Lead Consultants: G.K.A.K. Int. AB, Sweden
Interior Designers: Gregory Aeberhard PLC, London
Facade Lighting: Eletricité de France (EDF Paris)

Sheraton pre-opening office: PO Box 6002
Tel: (251-1) 517138 Fax: (251-1) 514029